THE
GLUTEN-FREE
QUICK BREADS
Cookbook

THE
GLUTEN-FREE
QUICK BREADS
Cookbook

75 Easy Homemade Loaves in *Half the Time*

SHARON LACHENDRO

creator of *What the Fork*

PAGE STREET
PUBLISHING CO.

PAGE STREET
PUBLISHING CO.

First published in 2019 by
Page Street Publishing Co.
27 Congress Street, Suite 105
Salem, MA 01970
www.pagestreetpublishing.com

Distributed by Macmillan, sales in Canada by The Canadian Manda Group.

23   22   21   20   19   1   2   3   4   5

ISBN-13: 978-1-62414-756-2
ISBN-10: 1-62414-756-9

Library of Congress Control Number: 2018955084

Cover and book design by Kylie Alexander for Page Street Publishing Co.
Photography by Sharon Lachendro

Printed and bound in China

TO ADAM – You are my North Star. My heart will always point to you.

TO KELSEY AND MACKENZIE– You can achieve anything you set your minds to. "I love you to the sun, the moon and the stars."

———

"May the sun bring you new energy by day,
May the moon softly restore you by night,
May the rain wash away your worries,
May the breeze blow new strength into your being.
May you walk gently through the world and know its
beauty all the days of your life."

—Apache Blessing

TABLE OF

CONTENTS ·········

INTRODUCTION

I've had my heart set on writing a baking cookbook for years. And here we are.

Some of the very first recipes that became popular on my blog were for my quick breads. I worked hard to create my own base recipes for gluten-free and dairy-free quick breads that could be tweaked here and there with different flavor combinations to create some stellar loaves for people with food intolerances. So, as you can imagine, I was pretty stoked to write an entire cookbook dedicated to that very subject.

This cookbook contains 75 amazing quick bread recipes that are all gluten-free and dairy-free and are quick and easy to make. Almost all of the recipes require little more than a couple of mixing bowls, a whisk and a spoon, and they use ingredients that are widely available. And since they're quick breads, there's no yeast or kneading involved!

If you've been missing breads and baked goods with the gluten-and-dairy-filled taste and texture that you remember, you need these recipes. They'll restore your faith in gluten-free baking and prove that gluten-free bread can be as good, if not better, than bread made with wheat flour.

Baking has always been a part of my life, long before this cookbook came to be. Some of my first memories are of watching my grandmother baking and kneading dough in her kitchen. To this day, the smell of yeast, dough and flour make me think of her and her Parker House Rolls.

I vividly remember watching my mom baking cookies, cakes and pies for family parties and holidays. I'd watch in amazement as she made perfectly flaky homemade pie crusts without even reading a recipe. It was all based on feel, and they were perfect every time.

They say the kitchen is where the heart is, and for me, that statement couldn't be truer. It's a gathering place; it's where the magic happens. The magic of combining the same ingredients with a few tweaks and different amounts of leavening agents and getting endless delicious results.

I started cooking and baking gluten-free in 2012 when my husband, Adam, discovered that he was gluten intolerant. As somebody who loved to cook and was already known among family and friends as the baker, I looked at this new and unexpected challenge as a huge obstacle, not knowing even where to start. You see, this was before I was familiar with food blogs, when gluten-free baking was still fairly uncommon (at least I thought so) and Pinterest was still relatively new, so recipe ideas were usually limited to over-the-top cheesy party foods, how to cook corn on the cob in a cooler, hedgehog cakes and a thousand ways to cook chicken breast.

Lucky for me, I wasn't alone in facing this challenge. My mom, the amazing baker, had already been eating gluten-free for years. She was instrumental in helping me figure out what gluten-free flours worked, making sure I knew to avoid using bean flours in baked goods, foods where we might find hidden sources of gluten, simple gluten-free swaps like using starch in place of flour to make gravy, and more. All of the basic things you need to know but might overlook because there's just so much to think about.

Over the years, I've taught myself even more about baking in general and experimented with different gluten-free flours and binding agents. I've gone through more gluten-free flour, sugar, avocado oil, eggs and sprinkles than I care to admit.

I'm someone who doesn't have to eat gluten-free, but I bake and cook for someone who does. I want everything that I make to have amazing taste and texture. I will not, and have not, settled for "just ok." I want my gluten-free quick breads and baked goods to be as good, if not better, than the original recipes that are made with gluten-filled flour. And that is exactly what these quick breads are.

Being able to eat gluten gives me a distinct advantage. I'm able to taste and compare my gluten-free baked goods and breads with ones made with regular wheat flour. I can assure you that the taste and textures are what they're meant to be without having to rely on what I think I remembered it to be ten years ago.

These gluten-free quick breads are good enough for gluten eaters. And if you don't tell them they're gluten-free and dairy-free, they probably won't even know. People might even tell you these are the best breads they've ever had and then you can knock their socks off and tell them your secret as you introduce them to the wonderful world of amazing gluten-free baking.

I hope you enjoy these quick bread recipes as much as my friends, family and I do. I've put everything I have and more into them.

Peace + Sweet Eats
xoxo,
Shay

MONKEY BUSINESS

SIMPLY DELICIOUS BANANA BREADS

There's nothing better than having a fresh-baked banana bread cooling on top of the oven. Banana breads are a staple in my house because they're so quick and easy to make, they're crazy delicious and we seem to always have overripe bananas hanging out on the counter. Honestly, I think I often buy extra just to have an excuse to bake with them.

My gluten-free banana bread has always been a popular recipe on my blog and I just had to include it here. It's Truly, the Best Ever Gluten-Free Banana Nut Bread (page 12)—try it and you'll see why! It's the foundation for all of the other banana breads in this chapter. They all showcase the banana flavor and really take it to the next level.

Feel free to experiment with some additional flavor combinations; I could have gone on and on but there are only so many recipes I can fit into one chapter! I recommend starting with the original banana bread recipe first, so you can see just how bangarang it is on its own. Then, work your way through the chapter. Your taste buds will thank you!

TRULY, THE BEST EVER GLUTEN-FREE BANANA NUT BREAD

2 cups (260 g) Sharon's Gluten-Free Flour Blend (page 179)

¾ tsp xanthan gum

1 tsp aluminum-free baking powder

½ tsp baking soda

½ tsp fine sea salt

½ cup (97 g) granulated sugar

½ cup (59 g) chopped walnuts

1 cup (230 g) mashed banana (about 2 medium)

2 large eggs, room temperature

½ cup (112 g) light brown sugar

⅔ cup (160 ml) walnut milk, room temperature

⅓ cup (80 ml) avocado oil

1 tsp pure vanilla extract

This gluten-free banana bread is insanely popular on my blog, and for good reason! It's got the perfect amount of moisture, it rises beautifully and the texture will trick you into thinking it's not actually gluten-free.

For the book version, I decided to play around with different nondairy milks. While I usually love baking with coconut milk, I've decided that I like walnut milk for this bread even more. Since this bread already has some walnuts mixed into the batter, it's a great way to really bring out that flavor. The walnut milk I use is slightly sweetened, so feel free to reduce the sugar in this bread a bit to suit your own taste preference. If you can't find walnut milk, just stick to unsweetened coconut milk. Either way, it's delicious!

Preheat the oven to 350°F (177°C). Coat a 9 x 5–inch (23 x 13–cm) loaf pan with homemade pan release (page 180), or spray it with nonstick spray and then line it with parchment paper.

In a large bowl, whisk together the gluten-free flour blend, xanthan gum, baking powder, baking soda, salt and granulated sugar. Stir in the walnuts, then set the mixture aside.

In a medium bowl, whisk together the mashed banana, eggs, brown sugar, walnut milk, oil and vanilla extract. Pour the wet ingredients into the dry ingredients, and stir until combined.

Transfer the batter into the prepared pan. Sprinkle the top of the banana bread with a few chopped walnuts if desired—no more than 1 to 2 tablespoons (7 to 14 g) total. Bake for 50 to 60 minutes or until a tester inserted into the middle of the loaf comes out clean.

Cool the bread in the pan for 20 minutes, then cool it completely on a wire rack.

STORAGE NOTE: Keep the bread wrapped tightly in plastic wrap at room temperature for up to 3 days. To freeze it, wrap it tightly in plastic wrap, then freeze it in a freezer-safe bag for up to 3 months.

CINNAMON SWIRL BANANA BREAD

FOR THE BREAD

2 cups (260 g) Sharon's Gluten-Free Flour Blend (page 179)

½ tsp xanthan gum

1 tsp aluminum-free baking powder

½ tsp baking soda

½ tsp fine sea salt

½ cup (97 g) granulated sugar

1 cup (230 g) mashed banana (about 2 medium)

2 large eggs, room temperature

¼ cup (55 g) light brown sugar, packed

⅔ cup (160 ml) unsweetened coconut milk, room temperature

⅓ cup (80 ml) avocado oil

1 tsp pure vanilla extract

FOR THE CINNAMON SWIRL

¼ cup (55 g) light brown sugar, packed

1 tbsp (8 g) ground cinnamon

NOTES: Keep the bread wrapped tightly in plastic wrap at room temperature for up to 3 days. To freeze it, wrap it tightly in plastic wrap, then freeze in a freezer-safe bag for up to 3 months.

Walnut milk can be used in place of the coconut milk in this recipe.

Cinnamon Swirl Bread meets Banana Bread for a flavor-filled mash-up that will make your taste buds happy. I've been making this family-favorite recipe for years but hadn't put it on the blog; I'd been saving it for a cookbook all this time. Finally, that time has come, and I can share it with you!

The brown sugar and cinnamon mixed with banana is such a wonderful combination. It's sweet with warm spices that are sure to quickly become a favorite. You'll always want to have overripe bananas on hand so you can make this any time the craving strikes. It's great warm or at room temperature.

Preheat the oven to 350°F (177°C) and spray a 9 x 5–inch (23 x 13–cm) loaf pan with nonstick spray or coat with homemade pan release (page 180). Line the long sides with parchment paper, leaving an overhang to pull the bread out of the pan.

In a large bowl, whisk together the gluten-free flour blend, xanthan gum, baking powder, baking soda, salt and granulated sugar. Set the mixture aside.

In a medium bowl, whisk together the mashed banana, eggs, brown sugar, coconut milk, oil and vanilla extract. Set the mixture aside.

To make the cinnamon swirl, in a small bowl, stir together the brown sugar and cinnamon and set the mixture aside.

Pour the wet ingredients into the dry ingredients. Mix until they're just combined. Pour half of the batter into the prepared baking pan.

Add two-thirds of the cinnamon mixture to the batter in the pan, sprinkling it evenly over the top. Top with the remaining batter, carefully smoothing it over the cinnamon mixture to cover it.

Sprinkle the remaining cinnamon mixture over the top of the batter and use a butter knife to gently swirl the cinnamon into the batter.

Bake for 50 to 60 minutes or until a cake tester or toothpick inserted in the middle comes out clean.

Cool the bread in the pan for 30 minutes, then use the parchment paper to remove the bread from the pan and finish cooling it on a wire rack.

CHOCOLATE HAZELNUT SWIRL BANANA BREAD

2 cups (260 g) Sharon's Gluten-Free Flour Blend (page 179)

¾ tsp xanthan gum

1 tsp aluminum-free baking powder

½ tsp baking soda

½ tsp fine sea salt

½ cup (97 g) granulated sugar

1 cup (230 g) mashed banana (about 2 medium)

2 large eggs, room temperature

½ cup (112 g) light brown sugar

⅔ cup (160 ml) unsweetened coconut milk, room temperature

⅓ cup (80 ml) avocado oil

1 tsp pure vanilla extract

½ cup (150 g) dairy-free chocolate hazelnut spread

Believe it or not, it's becoming easier to find dairy-free versions of chocolate hazelnut spread! Two prominent brands are Nutiva and Nocciolata. You can experiment with both and see which one you prefer; I usually use Nocciolata. I'm so happy to have found this product and basically want to bake with it all day, every day! It adds velvety smooth texture and an irresistible nutty-chocolate flavor to anything you make with it. And if you can find it, hazelnut milk would be great in this bread in place of the coconut milk. It'll really help to bring out the flavor and complement the chocolate hazelnut spread well.

Preheat the oven to 350°F (177°C). Coat a 9 x 5–inch (23 x 13–cm) loaf pan with homemade pan release (page 180), or spray it with nonstick spray, then line it with parchment paper.

In a large bowl, whisk together the gluten-free flour blend, xanthan gum, baking powder, baking soda, salt and granulated sugar. Set the mixture aside.

In a medium bowl, whisk together the mashed banana, eggs, brown sugar, coconut milk, oil and vanilla extract. Pour the wet ingredients into the dry ingredients, and stir until they're combined.

Add the chocolate hazelnut spread to a microwave-safe bowl and heat it for 20 seconds so it's just melted enough to drizzle/swirl.

Transfer half of the batter into the prepared pan. Top it with two-thirds of the chocolate hazelnut spread, distributing it evenly over the batter.

Add the remaining batter and then drizzle it with the remaining chocolate hazelnut spread. Use a knife to gently swirl the top of the bread.

Bake for 50 to 60 minutes or until a tester inserted into the middle of the loaf comes out clean.

Cool the bread in the pan for 20 minutes, then cool it completely on a wire rack.

STORAGE NOTE: Store the bread wrapped tightly in plastic wrap at room temperature for up to 3 days. To freeze it, tightly wrap the whole loaf, sliced or unsliced, in plastic wrap and place it in a freezer-safe bag. Freeze for up to 3 months.

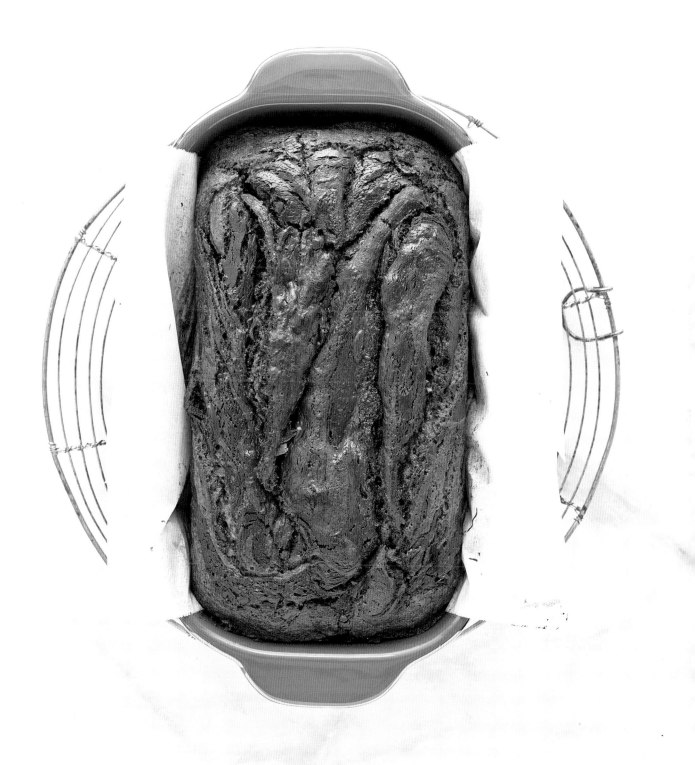

HUMMINGBIRD QUICK BREAD

2 cups (260 g) Sharon's Gluten-Free Flour Blend (page 179)

¼ tsp xanthan gum

½ cup (97 g) granulated sugar

1 tsp aluminum-free baking powder

½ tsp baking soda

½ tsp fine sea salt

1 tsp ground cinnamon

⅛ tsp ground allspice

½ cup (60 g) chopped pecans

1 cup (230 g) mashed banana (about 2 medium)

2 large eggs, room temperature

½ cup (115 g) crushed pineapple

½ cup (112 g) light brown sugar

½ cup (120 ml) unsweetened coconut milk, room temperature

⅓ cup (80 ml) avocado oil

1½ tsp (7 ml) pure vanilla extract

The timeless southern hummingbird cake is made with mashed banana, crushed pineapple and chopped pecans. This is a modern, gluten-free take on the classic cake. It's lighter and uses less sugar and oil, making it totally acceptable to serve for breakfast, brunch or afternoon tea! Feel free to use walnut milk in place of the coconut milk if you prefer. If you really want to make this bread a showstopper, top it with cream cheese icing (page 144) and dried pineapple flowers or extra chopped pecans.

Preheat the oven to 350°F (177°C) and coat a 9 x 5–inch (23 x 13–cm) loaf pan with homemade pan release (page 180) or spray it with nonstick spray, then line it with parchment paper.

In a large bowl, whisk together the gluten-free flour blend, xanthan gum, granulated sugar, baking powder, baking soda, salt, cinnamon and allspice. Stir in the pecans, then set the mixture aside.

In a medium bowl, whisk together the mashed banana, eggs, crushed pineapple, brown sugar, coconut milk, oil and vanilla extract. Pour the wet ingredients into the dry ingredients, and stir until they're combined.

Transfer the batter into the prepared pan. Bake for 55 to 65 minutes or until a tester inserted into the middle of the loaf comes out clean.

Cool the loaf in the pan for 20 minutes, then cool it completely on a wire rack.

STORAGE NOTE: Store the bread wrapped tightly in plastic wrap at room temperature for up to 3 days. To freeze it, tightly wrap the whole loaf, sliced or unsliced, in plastic wrap and place it in a freezer-safe bag. Freeze for up to 3 months.

THAT-ICE-CREAM-I-CAN'T-MENTION BREAD

2 cups (260 g) Sharon's Gluten-Free Flour Blend (page 179)

1 tsp xanthan gum

1 tsp aluminum-free baking powder

½ tsp baking soda

½ tsp fine sea salt

½ cup (97 g) granulated sugar

½ cup (59 g) chopped walnuts

½ cup (91 g) dairy-free chocolate chunks

1 cup (230 g) mashed banana (about 2 medium)

2 large eggs, room temperature

½ cup (112 g) light brown sugar

⅔ cup (160 ml) unsweetened coconut milk, room temperature

⅓ cup (80 ml) avocado oil

1 tsp pure vanilla extract

There's a famous banana ice cream flavor filled with fudge chunks and walnuts. I'm pretty sure you know which one I'm talking about. This bread was inspired by that ice cream flavor because chocolate, bananas and walnuts just go incredibly well together. I love being able to bring everyone's favorite dessert flavors into gluten-free, dairy-free recipes that can be enjoyed any time of the day. Feel free to use walnut milk in place of the coconut milk if you prefer. This is such an easy way to elevate a classic banana bread. You'll be making this version often, I'm sure!

Preheat the oven to 350°F (177°C) and coat a 9 x 5–inch (23 x 13–cm) loaf pan with homemade pan release (page 180) or spray it with nonstick spray.

In a large bowl, whisk together the gluten-free flour blend, xanthan gum, baking powder, baking soda, salt and granulated sugar. Stir in the walnuts and chocolate chunks, then set the mixture aside.

In a medium bowl, whisk together the mashed banana, eggs, brown sugar, coconut milk, oil and vanilla extract. Pour the wet ingredients into the dry ingredients, and stir until they're combined.

Transfer the batter into the prepared pan. Sprinkle the top of the banana bread with a few chocolate chunks and walnuts if desired—no more than 2 tablespoons (14 g) total. Bake for 55 to 65 minutes or until a tester inserted in the middle comes out clean.

Cool the loaf in the pan for 20 minutes, then cool it completely on a wire rack.

STORAGE NOTE: Store the bread wrapped tightly in plastic wrap at room temperature for up to 3 days. To freeze it, tightly wrap the whole loaf, sliced or unsliced, in plastic wrap and place it in a freezer-safe bag. Freeze for up to 3 months.

"CREAM CHEESE" SWIRL BANANA BREAD

FOR THE SWIRL

4 oz (113 g) dairy-free cream cheese, room temperature

1 large egg, room temperature

⅓ cup (65 g) granulated sugar

¼ cup (33 g) Sharon's Gluten-Free Flour Blend (page 179)

½ tsp pure vanilla extract

FOR THE BREAD

2 cups (260 g) Sharon's Gluten-Free Flour Blend (page 179)

¾ tsp xanthan gum

1 tsp aluminum-free baking powder

½ tsp baking soda

½ tsp fine sea salt

½ cup (97 g) granulated sugar

1 cup (230 g) mashed banana (about 2 medium)

2 large eggs, room temperature

½ cup (112 g) light brown sugar

⅔ cup (160 ml) walnut milk, room temperature

⅓ cup (80 ml) avocado oil

1 tsp pure vanilla extract

STORAGE NOTE:

Store the bread wrapped tightly in plastic wrap at room temperature for up to 3 days. To freeze it, tightly wrap the whole loaf, sliced or unsliced, in plastic wrap and place it in a freezer-safe bag. Freeze for up to 3 months.

With the increase of dairy-free products available, you can enjoy just about anything with a dairy-free substitute these days. This "cream cheese" may be dairy-free, but it's just as good as the real version, if not better! I use Daiya brand, but we also like Tofutti. The dairy-free cream cheese bakes up perfectly and forms a cheesecake-like filling in the bread—a deliciously sweet surprise! The walnut milk I use is slightly sweetened, so feel free to reduce the sugar in this bread a bit to suit your own taste. You can also use unsweetened coconut milk in place of the walnut milk.

Preheat the oven to 350°F (177°C) and coat a 9 x 5–inch (23 x 13–cm) loaf pan with homemade pan release (page 180) or spray it with nonstick spray, then line it with parchment paper.

To make the filling, add the dairy-free cream cheese and the egg to a medium bowl. Use a hand mixer to beat them together until they're smooth and creamy, about 1 to 2 minutes. Add the granulated sugar, gluten-free flour blend and vanilla extract. Beat the mixture for another minute until it's smooth. Set it aside.

To make the batter, whisk together the gluten-free flour blend, xanthan gum, baking powder, baking soda, salt and granulated sugar in a large bowl and set the mixture aside.

In a medium bowl, whisk together the mashed banana, eggs, brown sugar, walnut milk, oil and vanilla extract. Pour the wet ingredients into the dry ingredients and stir until combined.

Transfer half of the batter into the prepared pan. Add the cream cheese mixture and gently spread it over the batter, keeping it about ¼ to ½ inch (6 to 12 mm) from the sides. Top it with the remaining batter and smooth evenly.

Bake for 55 to 65 minutes or until a tester inserted in the middle of the loaf comes out clean.

Cool the loaf in the pan for 20 minutes, then cool it completely on a wire rack, removing the parchment paper.

PEANUT BUTTER BANANA BREAD

2 cups (260 g) Sharon's Gluten-Free Flour Blend (page 179)

¾ tsp xanthan gum

1 tsp aluminum-free baking powder

½ tsp baking soda

½ tsp fine sea salt

½ cup (97 g) granulated sugar

1 cup (230 g) mashed banana (about 2 medium)

2 large eggs, room temperature

½ cup (112 g) light brown sugar

⅔ cup (160 ml) unsweetened coconut milk, room temperature

⅓ cup (80 ml) avocado oil

1 tsp pure vanilla extract

½ cup (91 g) creamy peanut butter

If you've ever had a peanut butter banana sandwich, you know how great this flavor combination is. It's even better with an extra schmear of peanut butter on top! Dare I even suggest a drizzle of honey, too? Once you try this peanut butter banana bread, it might be hard to go back to regular banana bread.

Preheat the oven to 350°F (177°C) and coat a 9 x 5–inch (23 x 13–cm) loaf pan with homemade pan release (page 180) or spray it with nonstick spray, then line it with parchment paper.

In a large bowl, whisk together the gluten-free flour blend, xanthan gum, baking powder, baking soda, salt and granulated sugar. Set the mixture aside.

In a medium bowl, whisk together the mashed banana, eggs, brown sugar, coconut milk, oil and vanilla extract.

Add the peanut butter to a microwave-safe bowl and microwave it for 20 seconds, until it's melted enough to pour. Whisk it into the wet ingredients.

Pour the wet ingredients into the dry ingredients, and stir until they're combined.

Transfer the batter into the prepared pan. Bake for 50 to 60 minutes or until a tester inserted into the middle of the loaf comes out clean.

Cool the loaf in the pan for 20 minutes, then remove it from the pan and parchment paper to cool completely on a wire rack.

STORAGE NOTE: Store the bread wrapped tightly in plastic wrap at room temperature for up to 3 days. To freeze it, tightly wrap the whole loaf, sliced or unsliced, in plastic wrap and place it in a freezer-safe bag. Freeze for up to 3 months.

BLUEBERRY BANANA BREAD

2 cups (260 g) Sharon's Gluten-Free Flour Blend (page 179)

¾ tsp xanthan gum

1 tsp aluminum-free baking powder

½ tsp baking soda

½ tsp fine sea salt

½ cup (97 g) granulated sugar

½ tsp ground cinnamon, optional

1 cup (155 g) fresh blueberries

1 cup (230 g) mashed banana (about 2 medium)

2 large eggs, room temperature

½ cup (112 g) light brown sugar

⅔ cup (160 ml) unsweetened coconut milk, room temperature

⅓ cup (80 ml) avocado oil

1 tsp pure vanilla extract

While my husband usually reserves his best praise for recipes with chocolate or peanut butter, he raved about this bread. The blueberries really add a little something special to the usual banana bread. I almost always add some cinnamon to recipes with blueberries because I just love that flavor combination; I use it in my Blueberry Pecan Quick Bread (page 119) and Blueberry Muffin Bread (page 111). You can certainly omit it in this recipe if you prefer to have a more prominent banana flavor.

Preheat the oven to 350°F (177°C) and coat a 9 x 5–inch (23 x 13–cm) loaf pan with homemade pan release (page 180) or spray it with nonstick spray, then line it with parchment paper.

In a large bowl, whisk together the gluten-free flour blend, xanthan gum, baking powder, baking soda, salt, granulated sugar and cinnamon (if using). Gently stir in the fresh blueberries, then set the mixture aside.

In a medium bowl, whisk together the mashed banana, eggs, brown sugar, coconut milk, oil and vanilla extract. Pour the wet ingredients into the dry ingredients, and gently stir until they're combined.

Transfer the batter into the prepared pan. Bake for 50 to 60 minutes or until a tester inserted in the middle of the loaf comes out clean.

Cool the loaf in the pan for 20 minutes, then cool it completely on a wire rack.

STORAGE NOTE: Store the bread wrapped tightly in plastic wrap at room temperature for up to 3 days. To freeze it, tightly wrap the whole loaf, sliced or unsliced, in plastic wrap and place it in a freezer-safe bag. Freeze for up to 3 months.

ZUCCHINI BANANA BREAD

2 cups (260 g) Sharon's Gluten-Free Flour Blend (page 179)

¾ tsp xanthan gum

1 tsp aluminum-free baking powder

½ tsp baking soda

½ tsp fine sea salt

½ cup (97 g) granulated sugar

1½ tsp (4 g) ground cinnamon

½ cup (59 g) chopped walnuts

½ cup (115 g) mashed banana (about 1 medium)

2 large eggs, room temperature

½ cup (112 g) light brown sugar

½ cup (120 ml) walnut milk, room temperature

⅓ cup (80 ml) avocado oil

1 tsp pure vanilla extract

1 cup (100 g) grated zucchini

Two classic quick bread recipes collide! Bananas and zucchini work extremely well together in this quick bread taste sensation. This brings together the flavor of zucchini bread, with the combination of zucchini and cinnamon, and the flavor of banana bread, with the bananas and walnuts. It's such a perfect mash-up and is perfect for when you only have one overripe banana hanging out on the counter, begging to be baked. The walnut milk I use is slightly sweetened, so feel free to reduce the sugar in this bread a bit to suit your taste. Unsweetened coconut milk can also be used in place of the walnut milk.

Preheat the oven to 350°F (177°C) and coat a 9 x 5–inch (23 x 13–cm) loaf pan with homemade pan release (page 180) or spray it with nonstick spray, then line it with parchment paper.

In a large bowl, whisk together the gluten-free flour blend, xanthan gum, baking powder, baking soda, salt, granulated sugar and cinnamon. Stir in the walnuts, then set the mixture aside.

In a medium bowl, whisk together the mashed banana, eggs, brown sugar, milk, oil and vanilla extract.

Pour the wet ingredients into the dry ingredients, and stir until they're combined. Fold in the grated zucchini.

Transfer the batter into the prepared pan. Bake for 50 to 60 minutes or until a tester inserted into the middle of the loaf comes out clean.

Cool the loaf in the pan for 20 minutes, then cool it completely on a wire rack.

STORAGE NOTE: Store the bread wrapped tightly in plastic wrap at room temperature for up to 3 days. To freeze it, tightly wrap the whole loaf, sliced or unsliced, in plastic wrap and place it in a freezer-safe bag. Freeze for up to 3 months.

THE QUICK BREAD INSPIRED BY ELVIS

2 cups (260 g) Sharon's Gluten-Free Flour Blend (page 179)

¾ tsp xanthan gum

1 tsp aluminum-free baking powder

½ tsp baking soda

½ tsp fine sea salt

½ cup (97 g) granulated sugar

1 cup (230 g) mashed banana (about 2 medium)

2 large eggs, room temperature

½ cup (112 g) light brown sugar

⅔ cup (160 ml) unsweetened coconut milk, room temperature

⅓ cup (80 ml) avocado oil

1 tsp pure vanilla extract

½ cup (91 g) creamy peanut butter

½ cup (50 g) cooked and crumbled bacon

I feel like I should call this bread the King of All Quick Breads since it's inspired by the King himself. Elvis' favorite sandwich is a well-known phenomenon: peanut butter with bananas and bacon. This peanut butter banana bread with bacon is my quick bread nod to that sandwich. You can even spread yours with a bit of grape jelly, which is one of the ingredients in his other infamous sandwich, the Fool's Gold Loaf. Make sure not to use precooked or packaged bacon bits or crumbles as they are way too salty for this bread. Walnut milk can be used in place of the coconut milk if you prefer.

Preheat the oven to 350°F (177°C) and coat a 9 x 5–inch (23 x 13–cm) loaf pan with homemade pan release (page 180) or spray it with nonstick spray, then line it with parchment paper.

In a large bowl, whisk together the gluten-free flour blend, xanthan gum, baking powder, baking soda, salt and granulated sugar. Set the mixture aside.

In a medium bowl, whisk together the mashed banana, eggs, brown sugar, milk, oil and vanilla extract.

Add the peanut butter to a microwave-safe bowl and microwave it for 15 to 20 seconds until it's melted enough to pour. Whisk it into the wet ingredients.

Pour the wet ingredients into the dry ingredients, and stir until they're combined. Fold in the crumbled bacon.

Transfer the batter into the prepared pan. Bake for 50 to 60 minutes or until a tester inserted in the middle of the loaf comes out clean.

Cool the loaf in the pan for 20 minutes, then remove it from the pan and parchment paper to cool completely on a wire rack.

STORAGE NOTE: Store the bread wrapped tightly in plastic wrap at room temperature for up to 3 days. To freeze it, tightly wrap the whole loaf, sliced or unsliced, in plastic wrap and place it in a freezer-safe bag. Freeze for up to 3 months.

STRAWBERRY BANANA BREAD

¾ cup (15 g) freeze-dried strawberries

⅔ cup (160 ml) unsweetened coconut milk, room temperature

2 cups (260 g) Sharon's Gluten-Free Flour Blend (page 179)

¾ tsp xanthan gum

1 tsp aluminum-free baking powder

½ tsp baking soda

½ tsp fine sea salt

½ cup (97 g) granulated sugar

1 cup (230 g) mashed banana (about 2 medium)

2 large eggs, room temperature

½ cup (112 g) light brown sugar

⅓ cup (80 ml) avocado oil

1 tsp pure vanilla extract

Strawberry and banana is one of those classic fruity flavor combinations found basically everywhere you look. So, why not turn it into a quick bread, too? I use freeze-dried strawberries that are soaked in the milk before they're added to the bread. That turns the milk into strawberry milk (so good), and it also rehydrates the dried strawberries a bit so they're not chewy.

This bread is big on banana with a subtle strawberry flavor. If you want to amp up the strawberry flavor even more, you can add ¼ teaspoon (or a bit more to your liking) of strawberry extract. I prefer my bread without it.

Preheat the oven to 350°F (177°C) and coat a 9 x 5–inch (23 x 13–cm) loaf pan with homemade pan release (page 180) or spray it with nonstick spray, then line it with parchment paper.

Add the freeze-dried strawberries and coconut milk to a bowl. Stir to make sure all the strawberries are moistened/covered and set the mixture aside for at least 10 minutes.

In a large bowl, whisk together the gluten-free flour blend, xanthan gum, baking powder, baking soda, salt and granulated sugar. Set the mixture aside.

In a medium bowl, whisk together the mashed banana, eggs, brown sugar, oil and vanilla extract. Add the strawberries and coconut milk, and whisk to combine.

Pour the wet ingredients into the dry ingredients, and stir until all of the dry ingredients are incorporated.

Transfer the batter into the prepared pan and bake for 50 to 60 minutes or until a tester inserted in the middle of the loaf comes out clean.

Cool the loaf in the pan for 20 minutes, then cool it completely on a wire rack.

STORAGE NOTE: Store the bread wrapped tightly in plastic wrap at room temperature for up to 3 days. To freeze it, tightly wrap the whole loaf, sliced or unsliced, in plastic wrap and place it in a freezer-safe bag. Freeze for up to 3 months.

I DREAM IN CHOCOLATE

EASY QUICK BREADS TO CURB YOUR CRAVING

My prediction is that the breads in this chapter will be among your favorites, especially if you're a chocolate lover. These breads are a quick way to curb that chocolate craving. They're sweet enough for dessert but aren't too indulgent, so you can enjoy them with your afternoon coffee or tea. They come together faster than a cake, and they also have a little less sugar and oil than traditional cakes or other chocolate desserts. Sounds like an all-around win in my opinion!

This chapter all started with my Chocolate Quick Bread (page 36), a base recipe for every other bread in this chapter. Some of my personal favorites are the Chocolate Hazelnut Quick Bread (page 44), Mint Chocolate Quick Bread (page 43), Cold Brew Quick Bread with Coffee Glaze (page 39) and Chocolate Zucchini Bread (page 52). Anyone who loves the divine flavor combination of chocolate and peanut butter will love the Chocolate Peanut Butter Bread (page 48), and there's even an option for those who love chocolate and coconut together. While this chapter contains eleven breads, the sky is really the limit. Use the base recipe to create fun new flavor combinations with different mix-ins and glazes of your choice.

CHOCOLATE QUICK BREAD

1⅔ cups (220 g) Sharon's Gluten-Free Flour Blend (page 179)

1 tsp xanthan gum

⅓ cup (36 g) Dutch processed cocoa powder

½ cup (97 g) granulated sugar

1 tsp baking powder

½ tsp baking soda

½ tsp fine sea salt

2 large eggs, room temperature

¼ cup (55 g) light brown sugar

½–1 cup (123–245 g) vanilla or plain dairy-free yogurt, room temperature

⅔ cup (160 ml) unsweetened coconut milk, room temperature

⅓ cup (80 ml) avocado oil

1 tsp vanilla extract

½ tsp chocolate extract, optional (see recipe notes)

This quick bread is the foundation for all of the chocolate-based recipes in this book. It's a great blank canvas to experiment with flavor combinations and mix-ins to create fantastic loaves of sweet breads. You can vary the amount of dairy-free yogurt used in this recipe without affecting the taste. Using ½ cup (123 g) will yield a moist, yet firm loaf of bread, while using 1 cup (245 g) will yield a loaf with a softer, cakier texture. Both are equally good. I suggest experimenting with both amounts to see which you prefer. My family is split—I like the firmer bread because it's more "bread-like." My husband likes the cakier version.

Preheat the oven to 350°F (177°C) and coat a 9 x 5–inch (23 x 13–cm) loaf pan with homemade pan release (page 180) or spray it with nonstick spray, then line it with parchment paper.

In a large bowl, whisk together the gluten-free flour blend, xanthan gum, cocoa powder, granulated sugar, baking powder, baking soda and salt. Set it aside.

In a medium bowl, whisk together the eggs, brown sugar, dairy-free yogurt, coconut milk, oil, vanilla extract and chocolate extract, if using.

Pour the wet ingredients into the dry ingredients, and stir them until just combined. Transfer the batter to the prepared loaf pan and spread it evenly in the pan. Bake for 50 to 60 minutes depending on how much yogurt you used (see recipe notes) or until a cake tester inserted in the middle comes out clean.

NOTES: Store the bread wrapped tightly in plastic wrap at room temperature for up to 3 days. To freeze it, tightly wrap the whole loaf, sliced or unsliced, in plastic wrap and place it in a freezer-safe bag. Freeze for up to 3 months.

I use ½ teaspoon of chocolate extract to boost the chocolate flavor in this recipe. It's totally optional so if you don't have it, it's not a big deal. The cocoa powder still gives this a really nice rich, full chocolate flavor.

The more yogurt you use in the recipe, the longer it needs to bake. Using 1 cup (245 g) of yogurt will make the baking time closer to 60 minutes. Using ½ cup (123 g) will make it closer to 50 minutes.

COLD BREW QUICK BREAD WITH COFFEE GLAZE

FOR THE BREAD

1⅔ cups (220 g) Sharon's Gluten-Free Flour Blend (page 179)

1 tsp xanthan gum

⅓ cup (36 g) Dutch processed cocoa powder

½ cup (97 g) granulated sugar

1 tsp baking powder

½ tsp baking soda

½ tsp fine sea salt

2 large eggs, room temperature

¼ cup (55 g) light brown sugar

½ cup (123 g) vanilla or plain dairy-free yogurt, room temperature

⅔ cup (160 ml) cold brew coffee, room temperature

⅓ cup (80 ml) avocado oil

1 tsp vanilla extract

FOR THE GLAZE

1 cup (132 g) powdered sugar

1 tsp coffee extract

1 tsp pure vanilla extract

2 tsp (10 ml) cold brew coffee

This quick bread brings together two of my favorite things: cold brew coffee and chocolate. The satisfying chocolate flavor is perfectly complemented by the subtle hint of coffee. The glaze is a fun addition to the bread and makes it rival any treat you could get in a coffee shop. The coffee extract in the glaze packs a big punch without having to add a ton of liquid to achieve the same flavor. I find the coffee extract at my local grocery store in the baking aisle. You can even add a teaspoon of it to the bread if you want to really amp up that coffee flavor.

Preheat the oven to 350°F (177°C) and coat a 9 x 5–inch (23 x 13–cm) loaf pan with homemade pan release (page 180) or spray with nonstick spray. Line with parchment paper, then set aside.

In a large bowl, whisk together the gluten-free flour blend, xanthan gum, cocoa powder, granulated sugar, baking powder, baking soda and salt. Set it aside.

In a medium bowl, whisk together the eggs, brown sugar, dairy-free yogurt, cold brew coffee, oil and vanilla extract.

Pour the wet ingredients into the dry ingredients, and stir them until just combined. Transfer the batter to the prepared loaf pan and spread it evenly in the pan.

Bake for 50 to 60 minutes or until a cake tester comes out clean. Cool for 20 minutes in the pan, then remove from the pan and parchment paper to cool it completely on a wire rack.

When the bread is cool, whisk together the powdered sugar, coffee extract, vanilla extract and cold brew coffee. Stir this mixture until it's thin enough to drizzle on the bread, adding an additional teaspoon of cold brew coffee if needed.

Spread the glaze evenly on the top of the bread. Let the glaze set before slicing.

STORAGE NOTE: Store the bread wrapped tightly in plastic wrap at room temperature for up to 3 days. To freeze it, tightly wrap the whole loaf, sliced or unsliced, in plastic wrap and place it in a freezer-safe bag. Freeze for up to 3 months.

TRIPLE CHOCOLATE QUICK BREAD

This triple chocolate quick bread is truly meant for chocolate lovers. It has a deep, rich flavor and is full of dark chocolate chunks. Topped with a simple chocolate ganache, it's serious chocolate heaven. You can vary the amount of dairy-free yogurt used in this recipe without affecting the taste. Using ½ cup (123 g) will yield a moist, yet firm bread, while using 1 cup (245 g) will yield a loaf with a softer, cakier texture. I highly recommend using the full cup (245 g) in this recipe. While the ganache almost makes it a dessert, this bread tastes so great with coffee or tea; if you prefer this for a sweet breakfast, leave off the ganache and just go for a double chocolate bread.

FOR THE BREAD

1⅔ cups (220 g) Sharon's Gluten-Free Flour Blend (page 179)

1 tsp xanthan gum

⅓ cup (36 g) Dutch processed cocoa powder

½ cup (97 g) granulated sugar

1 tsp baking powder

½ tsp baking soda

½ tsp fine sea salt

1 cup (160 g) dairy-free dark chocolate chunks (I use Enjoy Life Foods)

2 large eggs, room temperature

¼ cup (55 g) light brown sugar

½–1 cup (123–245 g) vanilla or plain dairy-free yogurt, room temperature

⅔ cup (160 ml) unsweetened coconut milk, room temperature

⅓ cup (80 ml) avocado oil

1 tsp vanilla extract

FOR THE GANACHE

½ cup (95 g) semi-sweet dairy-free mini chocolate chips

¼ cup (60 ml) full-fat coconut milk

Preheat the oven to 350°F (177°C) and coat a 9 x 5–inch (23 x 13–cm) loaf pan with homemade pan release (page 180) or spray it with nonstick spray, then line it with parchment paper.

In a large bowl, whisk together the gluten-free flour blend, xanthan gum, cocoa powder, granulated sugar, baking powder, baking soda and salt. Stir in the chocolate chunks and set the mixture aside.

In a medium bowl, whisk together the eggs, brown sugar, dairy-free yogurt, coconut milk, oil and vanilla extract.

Pour the wet ingredients into the dry ingredients, and stir them until just combined. Transfer the batter to the prepared loaf pan and spread it evenly.

Bake for 50 to 60 minutes, depending on the amount of yogurt you used, or until a cake tester comes out clean. Cool before adding ganache.

To make the ganache, add the mini chocolate chips and coconut milk to a microwave-safe bowl. Melt the chocolate chips at 50 percent power for 60 seconds. Stir them well, then melt at 50 percent power for 20 seconds. Repeat in 10-second intervals if necessary until the chocolate is completely melted.

Pour the ganache over the cooled bread. Let it set for at least 30 minutes before slicing.

STORAGE NOTE: Store the bread at room temperature in an airtight container for up to 2 days. To freeze, slice into pieces and freeze flat on a sheet pan. When fully frozen, wrap in plastic wrap and transfer to a freezer-safe bag.

MINT CHOCOLATE QUICK BREAD

1⅔ cups (220 g) Sharon's Gluten-Free Flour Blend (page 179)

1 tsp xanthan gum

⅓ cup (36 g) Dutch processed cocoa powder

½ cup (97 g) granulated sugar

1 tsp baking powder

½ tsp baking soda

½ tsp fine sea salt

1 cup (160 g) dairy-free chocolate chunks

2 large eggs, room temperature

⅓ cup (75 g) light brown sugar

½ cup (120 ml) vanilla or plain dairy-free yogurt, room temperature

⅔ cup (160 ml) unsweetened coconut milk, room temperature

⅓ cup (80 ml) avocado oil

1 tsp peppermint extract

Mint and chocolate is a classic combination of flavors. While it's prevalent around holidays like Christmas and St. Patrick's Day, I say you should enjoy it any time of the year! Be sure to use peppermint extract here and not mint extract. I find that peppermint extract gives food a better flavor, while mint extract tastes more like spearmint, which reminds me of toothpaste or gum.

Want to take this bread even further? Top it with the chocolate ganache from the Triple Chocolate Quick Bread (page 40) and add ½ teaspoon of peppermint extract to it!

Preheat the oven to 350°F (177°C) and coat a 9 x 5–inch (23 x 13–cm) loaf pan with homemade pan release (page 180) or spray with nonstick spray. Line it with parchment paper, then set it aside.

In a large bowl, whisk together the gluten-free flour blend, xanthan gum, cocoa powder, granulated sugar, baking powder, baking soda and salt. Stir in the chocolate chunks and set the mixture aside.

In a medium bowl, whisk together the eggs, brown sugar, dairy-free yogurt, coconut milk, oil and peppermint extract.

Pour the wet ingredients into the dry ingredients, and stir them until just combined. Transfer the batter to the prepared loaf pan and spread it evenly in the pan.

Bake for 50 to 60 minutes or until a cake tester inserted in the middle comes out clean.

Cool the loaf on a wire rack for 20 minutes, then remove from the pan and parchment to cool it completely.

STORAGE NOTE: Store the bread wrapped tightly in plastic wrap at room temperature for up to 3 days. To freeze it, tightly wrap the whole loaf, sliced or unsliced, in plastic wrap and place it in a freezer-safe bag. Freeze for up to 3 months.

CHOCOLATE HAZELNUT QUICK BREAD

1⅔ cups (220 g) Sharon's Gluten-Free Flour Blend (page 179)

1 tsp xanthan gum

⅓ cup (36 g) Dutch processed cocoa powder

½ cup (97 g) granulated sugar

1 tsp baking powder

½ tsp baking soda

½ tsp fine sea salt

½ cup plus 1 tbsp (73 g) chopped hazelnuts, divided

2 large eggs, room temperature

¼ cup (55 g) light brown sugar

½ cup (123 g) vanilla or plain dairy-free yogurt, room temperature

⅔ cup (160 ml) unsweetened coconut milk, room temperature

⅓ cup (80 ml) avocado oil

1 tsp vanilla extract

⅓ cup (105 g) dairy-free chocolate hazelnut spread

Calling all Nutella fans! This bread is loaded with the flavors you love: the chocolate bread base is studded with chopped hazelnuts and swirled with dairy-free chocolate hazelnut spread. It's sweet and nutty, just like the spread itself. I use pre-chopped hazelnuts here—it makes prep a lot easier. Alternatively, you can roast and skin your own hazelnuts, but that takes a lot of extra time and effort. No need to be a kitchen hero; take the shortcut here. The faster you make this bread, the faster you can eat it.

Preheat the oven to 350°F (177°C) and coat a 9 x 5–inch (23 x 13–cm) loaf pan with homemade pan release (page 180) or spray with nonstick spray. Line with parchment paper, then set aside.

In a large bowl, whisk together the gluten-free flour blend, xanthan gum, cocoa powder, granulated sugar, baking powder, baking soda and salt. Stir in the chopped hazelnuts and set it aside.

In a medium bowl, whisk together the eggs, brown sugar, dairy-free yogurt, coconut milk, oil and vanilla extract.

Pour the wet ingredients into the dry ingredients, and stir them until just combined. Transfer the batter to the prepared loaf pan and spread it evenly in the pan.

Use a spoon to dollop the dairy-free chocolate hazelnut spread over the top of the batter. Use a butter knife to swirl it in, then top with the remaining 1 tablespoon (8 g) of chopped hazelnuts.

Bake for 50 to 60 minutes or until a cake tester inserted in the middle comes out clean. Cool the loaf in the pan for 20 minutes on a wire rack. Then remove it from the pan and parchment paper to cool it completely.

STORAGE NOTE: Store the bread wrapped tightly in plastic wrap at room temperature for up to 3 days. To freeze it, tightly wrap the whole loaf, sliced or unsliced, in plastic wrap and place it in a freezer-safe bag. Freeze for up to 3 months.

THAT-CANDY-BAR-I-CAN'T-MENTION BREAD

1⅔ cups (220 g) Sharon's Gluten-Free Flour Blend (page 179)

1 tsp xanthan gum

⅓ cup (36 g) Dutch processed cocoa powder

½ cup (97 g) granulated sugar

1 tsp baking powder

½ tsp baking soda

½ tsp fine sea salt

½ cup (38 g) shredded coconut

¼ cup (43 g) raw almonds, chopped

¼ cup (47 g) dairy-free mini chocolate chips

2 large eggs, room temperature

½ cup (112 g) light brown sugar

1 cup (245 g) vanilla or plain dairy-free yogurt, room temperature

⅔ cup (160 ml) unsweetened coconut milk, room temperature

⅓ cup (80 ml) avocado oil

1 tsp vanilla extract

OPTIONAL TOPPINGS

1 tbsp (15 g) dairy-free mini chocolate chips

1 tbsp (11 g) sliced almonds

1 tbsp (5 g) unsweetened coconut flakes

It's my favorite candy bar in quick bread form—you know, the one in the blue wrapper.

This chocolate-based quick bread is full of chopped almonds, shredded coconut and chunks of chocolate. I topped my quick bread with additional coconut and chocolate chunks. I also added sliced almonds to the top instead of chopped almonds. I think it makes a prettier presentation, especially if you're planning to gift this bread to someone. If you love that chocolate and coconut flavor combination, you'll definitely love it in this bread.

Preheat the oven to 350°F (177°C) and coat a 9 x 5–inch (23 x 13–cm) loaf pan with homemade pan release (page 180) or spray with nonstick spray. Line with parchment paper, then set aside.

In a large bowl, whisk together the gluten-free flour blend, xanthan gum, cocoa powder, granulated sugar, baking powder, baking soda and salt. Stir in the shredded coconut, chopped almonds and mini chocolate chips. Set it aside.

In a medium bowl, whisk together the eggs, brown sugar, dairy-free yogurt, coconut milk, oil and vanilla extract.

Pour the wet ingredients into the dry ingredients, and stir them until just combined. Transfer the batter to the prepared loaf pan and spread it evenly in the pan. Top the bread with mini chocolate chips, sliced almonds and unsweetened coconut flakes if you'd like.

Bake for 55 to 65 minutes or until a cake tester inserted in the middle comes out clean.

STORAGE NOTE: Store the bread wrapped tightly in plastic wrap at room temperature for up to 3 days. To freeze it, tightly wrap the whole loaf, sliced or unsliced, in plastic wrap and place it in a freezer-safe bag. Freeze for up to 3 months.

CHOCOLATE PEANUT BUTTER BREAD

1 ⅔ cups (220 g) Sharon's Gluten-Free Flour Blend (page 179)

1 tsp xanthan gum

⅓ cup (36 g) Dutch processed cocoa powder

½ cup (97 g) granulated sugar

1 tsp baking powder

½ tsp baking soda

½ tsp fine sea salt

2 large eggs, room temperature

¼ cup (55 g) light brown sugar

½ cup (123 g) vanilla or plain dairy-free yogurt, room temperature

¾ cup (180 ml) unsweetened coconut milk, room temperature

⅓ cup (80 ml) avocado oil

1 tsp pure vanilla extract

⅓ cup (60 g) creamy peanut butter

If you've ever read my blog, you probably know that the chocolate and peanut butter combination reigns supreme. It's my husband's favorite, and it's prevalent in my recipe archives. Naturally, this bread was a hit. It's got a smooth chocolate flavor with ribbons of creamy, salty peanut butter throughout. It's just sweet enough for our taste, but feel free to add an additional ¼ cup (55 g) of light brown sugar or some chocolate chips if you want it a bit sweeter.

Preheat the oven to 350°F (177°C) and coat a 9 x 5–inch (23 x 13–cm) loaf pan with homemade pan release (page 180) or spray with nonstick spray, then line with parchment paper.

In a large bowl, whisk together the gluten-free flour blend, xanthan gum, cocoa powder, granulated sugar, baking powder, baking soda and salt. Set the mixture aside.

In a medium bowl, whisk together the eggs, brown sugar, dairy-free yogurt, coconut milk, oil and vanilla extract. Set it aside.

Heat the peanut butter in a microwave-safe bowl for 10 to 20 seconds until it liquifies and is pourable. Set it aside.

Pour the wet ingredients into the dry ingredients and stir them until just combined. Transfer half of the batter to the prepared loaf pan and spread it evenly in the pan. Pour half of the melted peanut butter over the batter and gently swirl it with a butter knife.

Add the remaining batter and spread it evenly throughout the pan. Top with the remaining peanut butter and swirl it into the batter with a butter knife.

Bake for 50 to 60 minutes or until a cake tester inserted in the middle comes out clean. Cool in the pan on a wire rack for 20 minutes, then remove it from the pan and parchment paper to cool the bread completely.

STORAGE NOTE: Store the bread wrapped tightly in plastic wrap at room temperature for up to 3 days. To freeze it, tightly wrap the whole loaf, sliced or unsliced, in plastic wrap and place it in a freezer-safe bag. Freeze for up to 3 months.

CHOCOLATE AVOCADO BREAD

1⅔ cups (220 g) Sharon's Gluten-Free Flour Blend (page 179)

1 tsp xanthan gum

⅓ cup (36 g) Dutch processed cocoa powder

½ cup (97 g) granulated sugar

1 tsp baking powder

½ tsp baking soda

½ tsp fine sea salt

½ cup (95 g) dairy-free mini chocolate chips, plus 1 tbsp (15 g) for topping (optional)

2 large eggs, room temperature

½ cup (112 g) light brown sugar

1 cup (230 g) mashed avocado (about 1½ medium Haas avocados)

⅔ cup (160 ml) unsweetened coconut milk, room temperature

⅓ cup (80 ml) avocado oil

1 tsp vanilla extract

If you've never had chocolate and avocado together, don't be scared! It's actually a really amazing combo. Avocados have a distinct fruity flavor that pairs so well with chocolate. The first time I had chocolate and avocado together, I was hooked! Baking with chocolate and avocado is even better! This recipe calls for 1 cup (230 g) of mashed avocado, which is about one-and-a-half medium Haas avocados. You can blend the wet ingredients before adding to the dry ingredients if you prefer the bread to have no visible pieces of avocado. To save the other avocado half for later, leave it in the skin, brush it with some fresh lemon juice, wrap it tightly with foil and refrigerate it until you're ready to use it later in the day.

Preheat the oven to 350°F (177°C) and coat a 9 x 5–inch (23 x 13–cm) loaf pan with homemade pan release (page 180) or spray it with nonstick spray, then line it with parchment paper.

In a large bowl, whisk together the gluten-free flour blend, xanthan gum, cocoa powder, granulated sugar, baking powder, baking soda and salt. Stir in ½ cup (95 g) of chocolate chips, then set the mixture aside.

In a medium bowl, whisk together the eggs, brown sugar, mashed avocado, coconut milk, oil and vanilla extract.

Pour the wet ingredients into the dry ingredients, and stir until just combined. Transfer the batter to the prepared loaf pan and spread it evenly in the pan. Top with an additional 1 tablespoon (15 g) of chocolate chips if desired.

Bake for 50 to 60 minutes or until a cake tester inserted in the middle comes out clean.

Store the bread wrapped tightly in plastic wrap at room temperature for up to 3 days. To freeze it, tightly wrap the whole loaf, sliced or unsliced, in plastic wrap and place it in a freezer-safe bag. Freeze for up to 3 months.

CHOCOLATE ZUCCHINI BREAD

1⅔ cups (220 g) Sharon's Gluten-Free Flour Blend (page 179)

1 tsp xanthan gum

⅓ cup (36 g) Dutch processed cocoa powder

1 tsp baking powder

½ tsp baking soda

½ tsp fine sea salt

¾ cups (120 g) dairy-free chocolate chunks

2 large eggs, room temperature

⅔ cup (149 g) light brown sugar, packed

½ cup (120 ml) unsweetened coconut milk, room temperature

⅓ cup (80 ml) avocado oil

1 tsp pure vanilla extract

½ cup (123 g) vanilla or plain dairy-free yogurt, room temperature, optional

2 cups (200 g) grated zucchini

This Chocolate Zucchini Bread is an older recipe from my blog archives that I've brought back to life and updated for the cookbook. While the old version of the recipe was still very good, I've learned a ton about gluten-free baking over the last couple of years and I've also switched to baking with my own Gluten-Free Flour Blend (page 179) since I originally developed the recipe. I think this version has more chocolate flavor and a better texture. The yogurt is optional but adds more moisture. It's a real winner!

Preheat the oven to 350°F (177°C) and coat a 9 x 5–inch (23 x 13–cm) loaf pan with homemade pan release (page 180) or spray with nonstick spray. Line with parchment paper, then set aside.

In a large bowl, whisk together the gluten-free flour blend, xanthan gum, cocoa powder, baking powder, baking soda and salt. Stir in the chocolate chunks and set the mixture aside.

In a medium bowl, whisk together the eggs, brown sugar, coconut milk, oil, vanilla extract and dairy-free yogurt, if using.

Pour the wet ingredients into the dry ingredients, and stir them until just combined. Next, fold in the grated zucchini.

Transfer the batter to the prepared loaf pan and spread it evenly in the pan. Bake for 50 to 60 minutes or until a cake tester inserted in the middle comes out clean.

Cool the loaf in the pan on a wire rack for 20 minutes. Then remove it from the pan and parchment paper, and cool it completely on a wire rack.

STORAGE NOTE: Store the bread wrapped tightly in plastic wrap at room temperature for up to 3 days. To freeze it, tightly wrap the whole loaf, sliced or unsliced, in plastic wrap and place it in a freezer-safe bag. Freeze for up to 3 months.

CHOCOLATE PUMPKIN BREAD

1⅔ cups (220 g) Sharon's Gluten-Free Flour Blend (page 179)

1 tsp xanthan gum

⅓ cup (36 g) Dutch processed cocoa powder

½ cup (97 g) granulated sugar

1 tsp baking powder

½ tsp baking soda

½ tsp fine sea salt

1½ tsp (2½ g) Homemade Pumpkin Pie Spice (page 179)

2 large eggs, room temperature

½ cup (112 g) light brown sugar

1 cup (270 g) pumpkin puree

⅔ cup (160 ml) unsweetened coconut milk, room temperature

⅓ cup (80 ml) avocado oil

1 tsp vanilla extract

This is a really great base recipe that can be customized, so feel free to add up to 1 cup of your favorite mix-ins. Some great ones that I love are dairy-free chocolate chips or chunks and chopped pecans or walnuts. You can even take this a step further and top it with the chocolate ganache from the Triple Chocolate Quick Bread (page 40) or use the chocolate hazelnut swirl technique from the Chocolate Hazelnut Swirl Banana Bread (page 16). You can use homemade or canned pumpkin puree in this recipe, but if you're using canned, be sure it's plain pumpkin puree and not pumpkin pie filling.

Preheat the oven to 350°F (177°C) and coat a 9 x 5–inch (23 x 13–cm) loaf pan with homemade pan release (page 180) or spray it with nonstick spray, then line it with parchment paper.

In a large bowl, whisk together the gluten-free flour blend, xanthan gum, cocoa powder, granulated sugar, baking powder, baking soda, salt and pumpkin pie spice. Set the mixture aside.

In a medium bowl, whisk together the eggs, brown sugar, pumpkin puree, coconut milk, oil and vanilla extract.

Pour the wet ingredients into the dry ingredients, and stir them until just combined. Transfer the batter to the prepared loaf pan and spread it evenly in the pan.

Bake for 50 to 60 minutes or until a cake tester inserted in the middle comes out clean.

STORAGE NOTE: Store the bread wrapped tightly in plastic wrap at room temperature for up to 3 days. To freeze it, tightly wrap the whole loaf, sliced or unsliced, in plastic wrap and place it in a freezer-safe bag. Freeze for up to 3 months.

CHOCOLATE CHERRY PISTACHIO BREAD

1⅔ cups (220 g) Sharon's Gluten-Free Flour Blend (page 179)

1 tsp xanthan gum

⅓ cup (36 g) Dutch processed cocoa powder

½ cup (97 g) granulated sugar

1 tsp baking powder

½ tsp baking soda

½ tsp fine sea salt

½ cup (60 g) raw unsalted pistachios, chopped

2 large eggs, room temperature

⅔ cup (160 ml) unsweetened coconut milk, room temperature

¼ cup (55 g) light brown sugar

½ cup (123 g) vanilla or plain dairy-free yogurt, room temperature

⅓ cup (80 ml) avocado oil

1 tsp vanilla extract

1 cup (145 g) cherries, roughly chopped

One of my favorite snacks is a handful of pistachios, some fresh cherries and a little square of dark chocolate. I decided to turn that fun-flavored snack into a quick bread with delicious results! I didn't add chocolate chips since the bread is chocolate-based, but you could add a little without affecting the baking process if you'd prefer a chocolatier loaf. This bread isn't meant to be overly sweet, but you can add ¼ cup (55 g) more of light brown sugar if you prefer yours on the sweeter side. Fresh and frozen cherries both work here. If you use frozen cherries, be sure to defrost them first. If your frozen cherries give off a lot of liquid, you can use that cherry juice in place of some of the coconut milk.

Preheat the oven to 350°F (177°C) and coat a 9 x 5–inch (23 x 13–cm) loaf pan with homemade pan release (page 180) or spray with nonstick spray. Then line it with parchment paper and set it aside.

In a large bowl, whisk together the gluten-free flour blend, xanthan gum, cocoa powder, granulated sugar, baking powder, baking soda and salt. Stir in the chopped pistachios and set this mixture aside.

In a medium bowl, whisk together the eggs, coconut milk, brown sugar, dairy-free yogurt, oil and vanilla extract.

Pour the wet ingredients into the dry ingredients and stir them until just combined. Fold in the chopped cherries, then transfer the batter to the prepared loaf pan and spread it evenly in the pan.

Bake for 50 to 60 minutes or until a cake tester inserted in the middle comes out clean.

Cool the loaf in the pan on a wire rack for 20 minutes, then remove from the pan and parchment paper to cool completely.

STORAGE NOTE: Store the bread wrapped tightly in plastic wrap at room temperature for up to 3 days. To freeze it, tightly wrap the whole loaf, sliced or unsliced, in plastic wrap and place it in a freezer-safe bag. Freeze for up to 3 months.

I CAN'T BELIEVE IT'S NOT CAKE

BREADS INSPIRED BY CLASSIC CAKE FLAVORS

All of the breads in this chapter are based on—you guessed it—CAKE! I turned some classic cakes into quick breads by using less sugar and fat than you would in a traditional cake recipe, without sacrificing flavor. Another added bonus is that these breads are on the table and ready to eat in less time than a cake would take. These gluten-free and dairy-free quick breads are good enough to pass off as dessert, but I definitely won't judge if you choose to have them for breakfast. They are "breads," after all! All of the glazes and icings are optional add-ons. You can enjoy the full flavor of the breads without them, but the icings truly give you that cake-like experience.

BIRTHDAY CAKE QUICK BREAD

2 cups (260 g) Sharon's Gluten-Free Flour Blend (page 179)

1 tsp xanthan gum

1 tsp aluminum-free baking powder

½ tsp baking soda

½ tsp fine sea salt

1 cup (195 g) granulated sugar

¼ cup (43 g) gluten-free sprinkles

2 large eggs, room temperature

1 cup (240 ml) unsweetened coconut milk, room temperature

⅓ cup (80 ml) avocado oil

1 tsp pure vanilla extract

1 tsp butter extract

If you read my blog or have seen my Instagram account, you know that I'm a big fan of sprinkles. They're just so festive and fun, great for any occasion! I use a full ¼ cup (43 g) of gluten-free sprinkles here, so this loaf is jam-packed with color in every bite. Feel free to use a little less if you prefer. Avoid nonpareil sprinkles (the tiny round balls). They will bleed the color into the bread, turning it grey, which is not the look we're going for! The other main ingredient here, which is what truly makes it taste like birthday cake, is the butter extract. Don't skip it!

Preheat the oven to 350°F (177°C) and spray a 9 x 5–inch (23 x 13–cm) loaf pan with nonstick spray or coat with homemade pan release (page 180). Then line it with parchment paper and set it aside.

In a large bowl, whisk together the gluten-free flour blend, xanthan gum, baking powder, baking soda, salt and granulated sugar. Whisk in the sprinkles and set this mixture aside.

In a medium bowl, whisk together the eggs, coconut milk, oil, vanilla extract and butter extract.

Pour the wet ingredients into the dry ingredients. Mix until they're just combined, then transfer the batter to the prepared baking pan.

Bake for 50 to 60 minutes or until a tester inserted in the middle comes out clean. Cool it in the pan for 20 minutes, then remove the bread from the pan and parchment paper and allow it to cool on a wire rack.

STORAGE NOTE: Store the bread wrapped tightly in plastic wrap at room temperature for up to 3 days. To freeze it, tightly wrap the whole loaf, sliced or unsliced, in plastic wrap and place it in a freezer-safe bag. Freeze for up to 3 months.

CINNAMON SWIRL BREAD

This bread has been a longtime family favorite. It's loaded with cinnamon and brown sugar from the beautiful swirl in the middle and the cinnamon-sugar "crust" on top. Don't be afraid of the vinegar in this recipe. When combined with the other wet ingredients, it mimics buttermilk, just a dairy-free version! I promise you this bread won't taste like vinegar. Plus, there's so much cinnamon in this bread, that's pretty much all you'll taste, anyway—and that's a good thing!

FOR THE BREAD

2 cups (260 g) Sharon's Gluten-Free Flour Blend (page 179)

1 tsp xanthan gum

1 tsp aluminum-free baking powder

½ tsp baking soda

½ tsp fine sea salt

½ cup (97 g) granulated sugar

2 large eggs, room temperature

¼ cup (55 g) light brown sugar, packed

1 cup (240 ml) unsweetened coconut milk, room temperature

1 tbsp (15 ml) white vinegar

⅓ cup (80 ml) avocado oil

1 tsp pure vanilla extract

FOR THE CINNAMON SWIRL

¼ cup (55 g) light brown sugar, packed

1 tbsp (8 g) ground cinnamon

Preheat the oven to 350°F (177°C) and spray a 9 x 5–inch (23 x 13–cm) loaf pan with nonstick spray or coat with homemade pan release (page 180) and line the long sides with parchment paper, leaving an overhang to pull the bread out of the pan.

To make the bread, in a large bowl, whisk together the gluten-free flour blend, xanthan gum, baking powder, baking soda, salt and granulated sugar. Set it aside.

In a medium bowl, whisk together the eggs, light brown sugar, coconut milk, vinegar, oil and vanilla extract. Set this mixture aside.

To make the cinnamon swirl, in a small bowl, stir together the brown sugar and cinnamon. Set this aside.

Pour the wet ingredients into the dry ingredients. Mix until they're just combined. Pour half of the batter into the prepared baking pan.

Add two-thirds of the cinnamon mixture to the batter in the pan, sprinkling it evenly over the top. Top it with the remaining batter, carefully smoothing it over the cinnamon mixture to cover it.

Sprinkle the remaining cinnamon mixture over the top of the batter and use a butter knife to gently swirl the cinnamon into the batter.

Bake for 50 to 60 minutes or until a tester inserted in the middle comes out clean. Cool it in the pan for 30 minutes, use the parchment paper to remove the bread from the pan, then remove the parchment paper and allow it to cool on a wire rack.

STORAGE NOTE:

Store the bread wrapped tightly in plastic wrap at room temperature for up to 3 days. To freeze it, tightly wrap the whole loaf, sliced or unsliced, in plastic wrap and place it in a freezer-safe bag. Freeze for up to 3 months.

COCONUT BREAD

As a self-declared coconut fanatic, coconut cake has always been a favorite of mine. Naturally, I had to turn it into an epic quick bread that's just as flavorful but much easier to make than a full layer cake. I recommend using shredded sweetened coconut in this recipe as I find the unsweetened kind doesn't add enough sugary flavor. As with most of my other breads, the glaze is optional but a great addition if you're bringing this to a party or potluck, or giving it as a gift.

FOR THE BREAD

2 cups (260 g) Sharon's Gluten-Free Flour Blend (page 179)

1 tsp xanthan gum

2 tsp (7 g) aluminum-free baking powder

½ tsp fine sea salt

¾ cup (146 g) granulated sugar

1 cup (77 g) shredded coconut

2 large eggs, room temperature

1 cup (240 ml) full-fat coconut milk (from the can, stirred well)

⅓ cup (74 g) coconut oil, measured solid then melted

½ tsp coconut extract

½ tsp pure vanilla extract

FOR THE GLAZE

1 cup (132 g) powdered sugar

½ tsp coconut extract

½ tsp vanilla extract

1 tbsp (15 ml) unsweetened coconut milk

2 tbsp (10 g) toasted coconut flakes

Preheat the oven to 350°F (177°C) and spray a 9 x 5–inch (23 x 13–cm) loaf pan with nonstick spray or coat with homemade pan release (page 180). Then line the pan with parchment paper and set it aside.

In a large bowl, whisk together the gluten-free flour blend, xanthan gum, baking powder, salt and granulated sugar. Whisk in the shredded coconut and set this mixture aside.

In a medium bowl, whisk together the eggs, coconut milk, melted coconut oil, coconut extract and vanilla extract.

Pour the wet ingredients into the dry ingredients. Mix them until just combined, then transfer the batter into the prepared baking pan.

Bake for 50 to 55 minutes or until a cake tester or toothpick inserted in the middle comes out clean. Cool it in the pan for 20 minutes, then remove the bread from the pan and parchment paper and allow to cool completely on a wire rack.

To make the glaze, stir together the powdered sugar, coconut extract, vanilla extract and unsweetened coconut milk until they're smooth. Drizzle over the cooled bread and top it with the toasted coconut flakes. Let the glaze set before slicing.

STORAGE NOTES: Keep the un-glazed bread wrapped tightly in plastic wrap at room temperature for up to 3 days. To freeze, wrap tightly in plastic wrap, then freeze in a freezer-safe bag for up to 3 months.

To store the glazed bread, keep the bread covered in an airtight container. To freeze, slice the bread and freeze individual slices on a sheet pan. Then wrap individual slices in plastic wrap or transfer to sandwich bags before transferring to a freezer-safe bag. Remove the bread from plastic wrap before defrosting on a plate at room temperature.

CHOCOLATE CHIP QUICK BREAD

2 cups (260 g) Sharon's Gluten-Free Flour Blend (page 179)

¾ tsp xanthan gum

1 tsp aluminum-free baking powder

½ tsp baking soda

½ tsp fine sea salt

1 cup (195 g) granulated sugar

⅓ cup (67 g) dairy-free mini chocolate chips, plus 1 tbsp (15 g) for topping (optional)

2 large eggs, room temperature

1 cup (245 g) dairy-free plain or vanilla yogurt

½ cup (120 ml) unsweetened coconut milk, room temperature

⅓ cup (80 ml) avocado oil

1 tsp pure vanilla extract

My youngest frequently requests this bread—it's her absolute favorite out of all the recipes in this book. I think it's partly because she also loves to help me bake it (aka she's sneaking all the chocolate chips out of the bag when she thinks I'm not looking). This bread is moist and tender, thanks to the addition of yogurt. It mimics sour cream here, so if you're a fan of sour cream–based bread recipes, you'll want to give this one a try! I prefer using mini chocolate chips in this recipe. If you don't have them, regular chocolate chips will do—just use about ½ to ¾ cup (88 to 131 g) depending on how chocolatey you like it.

Preheat the oven to 350°F (177°C) and spray a 9 x 5–inch (23 x 13–cm) loaf pan with nonstick spray or coat with homemade pan release (page 180), then line it with parchment paper.

In a large bowl, whisk together the gluten-free flour blend, xanthan gum, baking powder, baking soda, salt and granulated sugar. Stir in the mini chocolate chips and set the mixture aside.

In a medium bowl, whisk together the eggs, dairy-free yogurt, coconut milk, oil and vanilla extract.

Pour the wet ingredients into the dry ingredients. Mix them until just combined, then transfer the batter to the prepared baking pan. Top it with the additional 1 tablespoon (15 g) of dairy-free mini chocolate chips if desired.

Bake for 50 to 60 minutes or until a cake tester or toothpick inserted in the middle comes out clean. Allow it to cool in the pan for 20 minutes, then remove the bread from the pan and parchment paper and cool on a wire rack.

STORAGE NOTE: Store the bread wrapped tightly in plastic wrap at room temperature for up to 3 days. To freeze it, tightly wrap the whole loaf, sliced or unsliced, in plastic wrap and place it in a freezer-safe bag. Freeze for up to 3 months.

RED VELVET QUICK BREAD

FOR THE BREAD

2 cups (260 g) Sharon's Gluten-Free
Flour Blend (page 179)

1 tsp xanthan gum

1 tbsp (7 g) unsweetened cocoa
powder

1 tsp aluminum-free baking
powder

½ tsp baking soda

½ tsp fine sea salt

1 cup (195 g) granulated sugar

2 large eggs, room temperature

1 cup (240 ml) unsweetened
coconut milk, room temperature

⅓ cup (80 ml) avocado oil

2 tsp (10 ml) white vinegar

1 tsp pure vanilla extract

1 tsp red food coloring

FOR THE CREAM CHEESE GLAZE

2 oz (58 g) dairy-free cream cheese,
room temperature

1 tbsp (12 g) palm shortening

1 tbsp (15 g) vegan butter

¾ cup (99 g) powdered sugar

¼ tsp pure vanilla extract

If you're a fan of all things red velvet, this quick bread needs to be on your list of recipes to try! Like the cake, this bread has a touch of cocoa powder. While my chocolate breads call for Dutch processed cocoa powder, I use regular unsweetened cocoa powder here, such as Hershey's. I chose to top it with a lighter, dairy-free cream cheese icing instead of a heavier cream cheese frosting because it's more fitting for bread. You can skip it, but it does make this bread more reminiscent of red velvet cake.

. . . .

Preheat the oven to 350°F (177°C) and spray a 9 x 5–inch (23 x 13–cm) loaf pan with nonstick spray or coat with homemade pan release (page 180). Then line it with parchment paper and set it aside.

In a large bowl, whisk together the gluten-free flour blend, xanthan gum, cocoa powder, baking powder, baking soda, salt and granulated sugar. Set the mixture aside.

In a medium bowl, whisk together the eggs, coconut milk, oil, vinegar, vanilla extract and red food coloring.

Pour the wet ingredients into the dry ingredients. Mix until they're just combined, then transfer the batter to the prepared baking pan.

Bake for 50 to 60 minutes or until a cake tester or toothpick inserted in the middle comes out clean. Cool the bread in the pan for 20 minutes, then remove the bread from the pan and parchment paper and cool on a wire rack. Allow the bread to cool completely before adding the dairy-free cream cheese glaze.

To make the glaze, add the dairy-free cream cheese, palm shortening, vegan butter, powdered sugar and vanilla extract to a medium bowl. Use a hand mixer to beat together until the mixture is smooth. Spread the glaze over the bread and let it set for 5 to 10 minutes before slicing it.

STORAGE NOTES: Keep the bread in an airtight container in the refrigerator for up to 2 days. Un-glazed bread can be kept at room temperature wrapped tightly in plastic wrap up to 3 days.

To freeze bread without the glaze, wrap tightly in plastic wrap then freeze in a freezer-safe bag for up to 3 months. To freeze bread with glaze, slice the bread, then freeze the slices on a baking sheet. Once frozen, wrap each slice in plastic wrap, then transfer to a freezer-safe bag and freeze up to 3 months. Thaw at room temperature before serving.

PIÑA COLADA BREAD

2 cups (260 g) Sharon's Gluten-Free Flour Blend (page 179)

¼ tsp xanthan gum

½ cup (97 g) granulated sugar

2 tsp (7 g) aluminum-free baking powder

½ tsp fine sea salt

2 large eggs, room temperature

½ cup (120 ml) canned full-fat coconut milk

½ cup (120 ml) cream of coconut

½ cup (135 g) canned crushed pineapple, undrained

⅓ cup (74 g) coconut oil, measured solid then melted

¼ cup (60 ml) pincapple juice

½ tsp coconut extract

½ tsp rum extract

1 tbsp (7 g) flaked coconut

Cherries, for garnish

Pull up a chair, put your feet up, close your eyes and pretend you are somewhere tropical while you're enjoying this Piña Colada Bread. The coconut and pineapple flavors shine; so, while you may not actually be on the beach, it will sure taste like it! I use canned, full-fat coconut milk in this recipe instead of unsweetened coconut milk. It's nice and thick and works so well with the pineapple and Piña Colada vibe. This recipe also calls for cream of coconut—I use the brand Coco Real because it comes in a squeeze bottle, making it easy to store for future use. I also use crushed pineapple canned in 100% juice, and I don't drain it before measuring it.

Preheat the oven to 350°F (177°C) and spray a 9 x 5–inch (23 x 13–cm) loaf pan with nonstick spray or coat with homemade pan release (page 180). Then line it with parchment paper and set aside.

In a large bowl, whisk together the gluten-free flour blend, xanthan gum, granulated sugar, baking powder and salt. Set this mixture aside.

In a medium bowl, whisk together the eggs, coconut milk, cream of coconut, crushed pineapple, melted coconut oil, pineapple juice, coconut extract and rum extract.

Pour the wet ingredients into the dry ingredients. Mix until they are just combined, then transfer the batter to the prepared baking pan. Top with the flaked coconut.

Bake for 50 to 60 minutes or until a cake tester or toothpick inserted in the middle comes out clean. Cool it in the pan for 20 minutes, then remove the bread from the pan, remove the parchment paper and allow to cool completely on a wire rack before slicing. Garnish with cherries.

STORAGE NOTE Store the bread wrapped tightly in plastic wrap at room temperature for up to 3 days. To freeze it, tightly wrap the whole loaf, sliced or unsliced, in plastic wrap and place it in a freezer-safe bag. Freeze for up to 3 months.

S'MORES BREAD

FOR THE BREAD

1½ cups (195 g) Sharon's Gluten-Free Flour Blend (page 179)

½ cup (40 g) gluten-free graham cracker crumbs, finely ground

1 tsp xanthan gum

1 tsp aluminum-free baking powder

½ tsp baking soda

½ tsp fine sea salt

2 large eggs, room temperature

¾ cup (168 g) light brown sugar

1 cup (240 ml) unsweetened coconut milk, room temperature

⅓ cup (80 ml) avocado oil

1 tsp pure vanilla extract

3 bars (96 g) Enjoy Life Foods rice milk chocolate

FOR THE GLAZE

½ cup (65 g) marshmallow fluff (or crème)

1 tsp coconut milk

My quick bread take on this classic treat is made with graham cracker "flour" and has "milk chocolate" sandwiched between the loaf layers. It's topped with a sweet marshmallow glaze, making the s'mores effect complete. The chocolate bars I use are made with rice milk and taste very similar to milk chocolate. You could use dark chocolate instead, but the rice milk bars really give it that true s'mores taste. If you have a kitchen torch, feel free to toast up the marshmallow glaze with it. You could also put it under the broiler for a minute, but watch it very closely so it doesn't burn. This would be a fun bread to take along camping or on a road trip!

Preheat the oven to 350°F (177°C) and spray a 9 x 5–inch (23 x 13–cm) loaf pan with nonstick spray or coat with homemade pan release (page 180). Then line it with parchment paper and set it aside.

In a large bowl, whisk together the gluten-free flour blend, graham cracker crumbs, xanthan gum, baking powder, baking soda and salt. Set this mixture aside.

In a medium bowl, whisk together the eggs, light brown sugar, coconut milk, oil and vanilla extract.

Pour the wet ingredients into the dry ingredients, and mix them until just combined. Pour half of the batter into the prepared baking pan. Top with the 3 chocolate bars, breaking one in half so that it fits. Cover with the remaining batter.

Bake for 50 to 60 minutes or until a cake tester or toothpick inserted in the middle comes out clean. Cool the bread in the pan for 20 minutes, then remove the bread from the pan and parchment paper and cool it completely on a wire rack.

To make the glaze, whisk together the marshmallow fluff and coconut milk until they are combined. Drizzle the glaze over the cooled bread.

STORAGE NOTE: Keep the bread in an airtight container at room temperature for up to 3 days. To freeze it, tightly wrap the whole loaf, sliced or unsliced, in plastic wrap and place it in a freezer-safe bag. Freeze for up to 3 months. I do not recommend freezing this bread with the glaze.

VANILLA BEAN BREAD

2 cups (260 g) Sharon's Gluten-Free Flour Blend (page 179)

1 tsp xanthan gum

1 tsp aluminum-free baking powder

½ tsp baking soda

½ tsp fine sea salt

1 cup (195 g) granulated sugar

2 large eggs, room temperature

1 cup (240 ml) unsweetened coconut milk, room temperature

⅓ cup (80 ml) avocado oil

1 tbsp (15 ml) vanilla bean paste or seeds from 1 vanilla bean pod

This is the base recipe for many of the breads in this book. While it may seem rather plain, it's anything but boring! It's got a nice, sweet taste and is speckled with gorgeous vanilla bean flecks. I use vanilla bean paste because it's readily available, but you can also scrape the seeds out of a vanilla bean instead. Don't have vanilla bean paste or vanilla beans? Just use a full tablespoon (15 ml) of pure vanilla extract instead. The flavor will be subtler, and the bread won't have that vanilla bean look, but it will still taste amazing!

Preheat the oven to 350°F (177°C) and spray a 9 x 5–inch (23 x 13–cm) loaf pan with nonstick spray or coat with homemade pan release (page 180). Then line it with parchment paper and set it aside.

In a large bowl, whisk together the gluten-free flour blend, xanthan gum, baking powder, baking soda, salt and granulated sugar. Set this mixture aside.

In a medium bowl, whisk together the eggs, coconut milk, oil and vanilla bean paste.

Pour the wet ingredients into the dry ingredients. Mix them until they're just combined, then transfer the batter to the prepared baking pan.

Bake for 50 to 60 minutes or until a cake tester or toothpick inserted in the middle comes out clean. Cool it in the pan for 20 minutes, then remove the bread from the pan and parchment paper and allow to cool on a wire rack.

STORAGE NOTE: Store the bread wrapped tightly in plastic wrap at room temperature for up to 3 days. To freeze it, tightly wrap the whole loaf, sliced or unsliced, in plastic wrap and place it in a freezer-safe bag. Freeze for up to 3 months.

ALMOND POPPY SEED BREAD

FOR THE BREAD

2 cups (260 g) Sharon's Gluten-Free Flour Blend (page 179)

1 tsp xanthan gum

2 tsp (7 g) aluminum-free baking powder

½ tsp baking soda

½ tsp fine sea salt

1 cup (195 g) granulated sugar

1 tbsp (9 g) poppy seeds

2 large eggs, room temperature

1 cup (240 ml) unsweetened coconut milk, room temperature

⅓ cup (80 ml) avocado oil

1 tbsp (15 ml) white vinegar

1½ tsp (7 ml) almond extract

½ tsp pure vanilla extract

FOR THE GLAZE (OPTIONAL)

1 cup (132 g) powdered sugar

½ tsp almond extract

½ tsp vanilla extract

1 tbsp (15 ml) unsweetened coconut milk

This recipe was one I tested about halfway through writing this book, which means I had already baked more than 30 different flavors of bread, including many, many banana breads and chocolate breads. So, when my chocolate-loving husband declared this his "dark horse favorite," I was honestly shocked. There wasn't an ounce of chocolate in sight. He said it reminds him of the shortbread cookies he used to eat before going gluten-free.

Preheat the oven to 350°F (177°C) and spray a 9 x 5–inch (23 x 13–cm) loaf pan with nonstick spray or coat with homemade pan release (page 180). Then line it with parchment paper and set it aside.

In a large bowl, whisk together the gluten-free flour blend, xanthan gum, baking powder, baking soda, salt and granulated sugar. Whisk in the poppy seeds and set the mixture aside.

In a medium bowl, whisk together the eggs, coconut milk, oil, vinegar, almond extract and vanilla extract.

Pour the wet ingredients into the dry ingredients. Mix them until just combined and then transfer the batter to the prepared baking pan.

Bake for 50 to 55 minutes or until a cake tester or toothpick inserted in the middle comes out clean. Cool the bread in the pan for 30 minutes, then remove the bread from the pan and parchment paper and allow it to cool completely on a wire rack.

To make the glaze, stir together the powdered sugar, almond extract, vanilla extract and unsweetened coconut milk until it's smooth. Drizzle the glaze over the cooled bread and let it set before slicing.

STORAGE NOTES: Store the unglazed bread wrapped tightly in plastic wrap at room temperature for up to 3 days. To freeze it, tightly wrap the whole loaf, sliced or unsliced, in plastic wrap and place it in a freezer-safe bag. Freeze for up to 3 months.

To store the glazed bread, keep the bread covered in an airtight container. To freeze, slice the bread and freeze individual slices on a sheet pan. Then wrap individual slices in plastic wrap or transfer to sandwich bags before transferring to a freezer-safe bag. Remove the bread from plastic wrap before defrosting on a plate at room temperature.

CHERRY CHIP MINI BREADS

I originally made this recipe as one big loaf, but I like it better in mini form. They're just so cute and petite! Plus, that fun pink glaze and pink-tinged bread is just begging to be made into minis. They're perfect for parties and special occasions. There's something about the color pink that just makes you want to celebrate! If you prefer a full-sized loaf, you can bake this in a 9 x 5–inch (23 x 13–cm) pan for 50 to 60 minutes.

FOR THE BREAD

2 cups plus 1 tbsp (269 g) Sharon's Gluten-Free Flour Blend (page 179), divided

1 tsp xanthan gum

1 cup (195 g) granulated sugar

2 tsp (7 g) aluminum-free baking powder

½ tsp fine sea salt

1 (10-oz [284-g]) jar maraschino cherries, chopped, juice reserved

2 large eggs, room temperature

½ cup (120 ml) unsweetened coconut milk, room temperature

½ cup (120 ml) reserved maraschino cherry juice

⅓ cup (80 ml) avocado oil

1½ tsp (7 ml) almond extract

FOR THE GLAZE

1 cup (132 g) powdered sugar

1 tbsp (15 ml) reserved maraschino cherry juice

1 tsp almond extract

1 tsp unsweetened coconut milk, plus more as needed

Preheat the oven to 350°F (177°C) and spray 4 standard mini loaf pans with nonstick spray or coat with homemade pan release (page 180). Then line with parchment paper and set aside.

In a large bowl, whisk together 2 cups (260 g) of gluten-free flour blend, xanthan gum, granulated sugar, baking powder and salt. Set it aside.

Combine the cherries and 1 tablespoon (9 g) of gluten-free flour blend in a small bowl. Set this aside.

In a medium bowl, whisk together the eggs, coconut milk, reserved cherry juice, oil and almond extract.

Pour the wet ingredients into the dry ingredients. Mix until they're just combined, then transfer the batter to the prepared baking pans, dividing it evenly.

Bake for 35 to 45 minutes or until a cake tester or toothpick inserted in the middle comes out clean. Cool in the pans for 10 minutes, then transfer to a wire rack. Cool breads completely before adding the glaze.

To make the glaze, stir together the powdered sugar, reserved cherry juice and almond extract. Add unsweetened coconut milk, thinning the glaze enough to drizzle on the breads. Add more, 1 teaspoon at a time, to reach your desired consistency.

STORAGE NOTES: Keep the breads in an airtight container at room temperature for up to 3 days. If breads aren't glazed, they can be wrapped in plastic wrap. To freeze, wrap un-glazed breads tightly in plastic wrap, then freeze in a freezer-safe bag for up to 3 months.

If glazed, freeze on a sheet pan. Once fully frozen, wrap individual breads in plastic wrap and transfer to a freezer bag. Unwrap and defrost at room temperature.

CARROT CAKE QUICK BREAD

This bread tastes exactly like carrot cake, but requires way less work, time, sugar and oil than the dessert version. This also has my go-to carrot cake ingredients: shredded coconut, chopped walnuts and crushed pineapple. You can swap pecans for the walnuts, just don't skip the pineapple and coconut!

FOR THE BREAD

2 cups (260 g) Sharon's Gluten-Free Flour Blend (page 179)

¼ tsp xanthan gum

1 cup (195 g) granulated sugar

1 tsp aluminum-free baking powder

½ tsp baking soda

½ tsp fine sea salt

1 tsp ground cinnamon

½ cup (59 g) chopped walnuts

¼ cup (25 g) shredded coconut

2 large eggs, room temperature

⅔ cup (160 ml) unsweetened coconut milk, room temperature

⅓ cup (80 ml) avocado oil

1½ tsp (7 ml) pure vanilla extract

½ cup (135 g) crushed pineapple in juice

1 cup (110 g) grated carrot

FOR THE ICING

1 tbsp (15 g) vegan butter

1 tbsp (12 g) shortening

2 oz (58 g) dairy-free cream cheese

¾ cup (99 g) powdered sugar

¼ tsp vanilla extract

Preheat the oven to 350°F (177°C) and spray a 9 x 5–inch (23 x 13–cm) loaf pan with nonstick spray or coat with homemade pan release (page 180), then line it with parchment paper.

In a large bowl, whisk together the gluten-free flour blend, xanthan gum, granulated sugar, baking powder, baking soda, salt and cinnamon. Stir in the walnuts and coconut, then set the mixture aside.

In a medium bowl, whisk together the eggs, coconut milk, oil, vanilla extract and pineapple.

Pour the wet ingredients into the dry ingredients. Mix them until just combined and then fold in the grated carrot.

Transfer the batter to the prepared baking pan. Bake for 50 to 60 minutes or until a cake tester or toothpick inserted in the middle comes out clean.

Cool in the pan for 20 minutes, then cool on a wire rack before adding the icing.

To make the icing, add the vegan butter, shortening and dairy-free cream cheese to a medium bowl. Beat with an electric hand mixer until completely combined. Add the powdered sugar and the vanilla extract. Beat until smooth, then spread on top of the bread.

STORAGE NOTES: Store the bread in an airtight container at room temperature for up to 2 days. To freeze without the icing, tightly wrap the whole loaf, sliced or unsliced, in plastic wrap and place it in a freezer-safe bag. Freeze for up to 3 months.

To freeze with the icing, slice and place bread flat on a sheet pan and freeze until solid. Wrap each slice in plastic wrap and store in a freezer-safe bag. Unwrap and defrost at room temperature.

EASY-PEASY, LEMON . . .

FRESH CITRUS BREADS

I love to start baking citrus breads in the winter, shortly after the charm of fresh snow and the high of Christmas has worn off. It makes me feel like we're ever so slightly closer to spring, sunshine and fresh blooms. However, living in New England means that the arrival of spring is still way, way off for me. With these quick and effortless recipes, at least I can pretend the warmer weather is already here. The tequila in the Margarita Bread (page 88) will transport you from a snowy landscape to a beach-side cabana, and the Loaded Lemon Bread (page 91) will have you longing for summer days spent sipping lemonade by the pool.

This chapter is full of easy, bright, fresh-flavored gluten-free and dairy-free loaves to help you ward off those winter blues and cabin fever. But don't hold back because of the season! The availability of fresh produce makes these breads great to make any time of the year.

CLASSIC LEMON BREAD WITH LEMON GLAZE

FOR THE BREAD

1 cup (195 g) granulated sugar

Zest from 1 lemon

2 cups (260 g) Sharon's Gluten-Free Flour Blend (page 179)

¼ tsp xanthan gum

2 tsp (7 g) aluminum-free baking powder

½ tsp fine sea salt

2 large eggs, room temperature

¾ cup (180 ml) unsweetened coconut milk, room temperature

⅓ cup (80 ml) avocado oil

Juice from 1 lemon

1 tbsp (15 ml) lemon extract

1 tsp pure vanilla extract

3–5 drops yellow food coloring, optional

FOR THE GLAZE

1 cup (132 g) powdered sugar

Zest from 1 medium lemon

Juice from 1 lemon (about 2 tbsp [30 ml])

*This recipe took more tries than I'd care to admit to get it right. But this loaf is so good, it was worth it. It gets its flavor from four sources of lemon—the zest, juice, extract and glaze. The extract is essential and **cannot** be replaced with more fresh lemon juice. The acidity will negatively react with the starches in my gluten-free flour blend, making the bread rubbery. Concentrated lemon juice from the bottle also won't work, so be sure to follow this recipe exactly to achieve the best results.*

Preheat the oven to 350°F (177°C) and spray a 9 x 5–inch (23 x 13–cm) loaf pan with nonstick spray or coat with homemade pan release (page 180). Then line it with parchment paper and set aside.

Add the granulated sugar and lemon zest to a large bowl. Rub the zest into the sugar to help release the natural oils. Add the gluten-free flour blend, xanthan gum, baking powder and salt. Whisk them until they're combined, and then set it aside.

In a medium bowl, whisk together the eggs, coconut milk, oil, lemon juice, lemon extract and vanilla extract. Whisk in the food coloring if you're using it.

Pour the wet ingredients into the dry ingredients. Mix until they're just combined, then transfer the batter to the prepared baking pan.

Bake for 50 to 60 minutes or until a cake tester or toothpick inserted in the middle comes out clean. Cool the bread in the pan for 30 minutes, then remove the bread from the pan and cool completely on a wire rack. Allow it to cool completely before adding the glaze.

To make the glaze, add the powdered sugar, lemon zest and lemon juice to a bowl and stir until combined. If the glaze is too thick, add 1 teaspoon of unsweetened coconut milk at a time until it's thin enough to drizzle/spread.

STORAGE NOTES: Keep the bread covered in an airtight container at room temperature for up to 3 days. To freeze glazed bread, slice into individual pieces, then freeze flat on a sheet pan. Transfer the slices to a freezer-safe bag with wax paper between each piece. Defrost at room temperature.

To freeze the bread without glaze, wrap tightly in plastic wrap, then freeze in a freezer-safe bag for up to 3 months.

RASPBERRY LEMONADE BREAD

2 cups (260 g) Sharon's Gluten-Free Flour Blend (page 179)

1 tsp xanthan gum

⅔ cup (130 g) granulated sugar

1 tsp aluminum-free baking powder

½ tsp baking soda

½ tsp fine sea salt

1 cup (240 ml) water

2 rounded tbsp (34 g) lemonade mix

2 large eggs, room temperature

⅓ cup (80 ml) avocado oil

1 tsp vanilla extract

½ tsp lemon extract

1 cup (115 g) fresh raspberries

I love taking a classic flavor pairing and turning it into something unexpected like a baked good. This bread does exactly that. Raspberry lemonade is a beloved summer drink. It's light, refreshing, slightly sweet and a little tart all at the same time. This quick bread brings that flavor in loaf form with lemonade mix and fresh red raspberries. Live life to its sweet potential with a glass of raspberry lemonade in one hand and a slice of this bread in the other.

Preheat the oven to 350°F (177°C) and spray a 9 x 5–inch (23 x 13–cm) loaf pan with nonstick spray or coat with homemade pan release (page 180). Then line with parchment paper and set aside.

In a large bowl, whisk together the gluten-free flour blend, xanthan gum, granulated sugar, baking powder, baking soda and salt.

In a medium bowl, whisk together the water and lemonade mix until the lemonade mix is dissolved. Whisk in the eggs, oil, vanilla extract and lemon extract.

Pour the wet ingredients into the dry ingredients. Mix them until just combined, then gently fold in the raspberries.

Transfer the batter to the prepared baking pan.

Bake for 50 to 60 minutes or until a cake tester or toothpick inserted in the middle comes out clean. Cool the bread in the pan for 20 minutes, then remove the bread from the pan, remove the parchment paper and cool on a wire rack.

STORAGE NOTE: Store the bread wrapped tightly in plastic wrap at room temperature for up to 3 days. To freeze it, tightly wrap the whole loaf, sliced or unsliced, in plastic wrap and place it in a freezer-safe bag. Freeze for up to 3 months.

MARGARITA BREAD

You have probably seen margarita-inspired cupcakes, pies and other desserts. But have you ever had a margarita bread? Like the drink, this quick bread gets its flavor from fresh limes and tequila. There's only 2 tablespoons (30 ml) of tequila in this recipe, just enough to get that flavor profile. I use silver tequila, but gold would be fine, too. Just before serving this bread, hit it with a small sprinkle of margarita salt for the ultimate cocktail-inspired experience!

FOR THE BREAD

1 cup (195 g) granulated sugar

1 tbsp (6 g) lime zest (from 2 small limes)

2 cups (260 g) Sharon's Gluten-Free Flour Blend (page 179)

½ tsp xanthan gum

1 tsp aluminum-free baking powder

½ tsp baking soda

½ tsp fine sea salt

2 large eggs, room temperature

⅔ cup (160 ml) unsweetened coconut milk, room temperature

⅓ cup (80 ml) avocado oil

1 tsp pure vanilla extract

2 tbsp (30 ml) fresh lime juice (from 2 small limes)

2 tbsp (30 ml) tequila

FOR THE GLAZE

1 cup (132 g) powdered sugar

Zest from 1 lime

Juice from 1 lime, or about 2 tbsp (30 ml)

Margarita salt, for serving

Preheat the oven to 350°F (177°C) and spray a 9 x 5–inch (23 x 13–cm) loaf pan with nonstick spray or coat with homemade pan release (page 180). Then line it with parchment paper and set aside.

In a large bowl, add the granulated sugar and lime zest. Use your fingers to rub the zest into the sugar to help release the natural oils. Add the gluten-free flour blend, xanthan gum, baking powder, baking soda and salt. Whisk them together and set the mixture aside.

In a medium bowl, whisk together the eggs, coconut milk, oil, vanilla extract, lime juice and tequila.

Pour the wet ingredients into the dry ingredients. Mix them until just combined, then transfer the batter to the prepared baking pan.

Bake for 50 to 60 minutes or until a cake tester or toothpick inserted in the middle comes out clean. Cool in the pan for 20 minutes, then cool it completely on a wire rack before adding the glaze.

To make the glaze, add the powdered sugar, lime zest and lime juice to a bowl. Stir until smooth and just thin enough to drizzle. If the glaze is too thick, add 1 teaspoon of unsweetened coconut milk at a time until it's thin enough to drizzle. If your glaze is too thin, add a little powdered sugar.

Just before serving, sprinkle a pinch of margarita salt over the glaze after it has set. Adjust the salt to taste.

STORAGE NOTES: Keep the bread covered in an airtight container at room temperature for up to 3 days. To freeze the glazed bread, slice into individual pieces, then freeze flat on a sheet pan. Transfer the frozen slices to a freezer-safe bag with wax paper between each piece. Defrost at room temperature.

To freeze the bread without glaze, wrap tightly in plastic wrap, then freeze in a freezer-safe bag for up to 3 months.

LOADED LEMON BREAD
(AKA THE MODERN FRUITCAKE)

1 cup (195 g) granulated sugar

Zest from 1 lemon

2 cups (260 g) Sharon's Gluten-Free Flour Blend (page 179)

½ tsp xanthan gum

2 tsp (7 g) aluminum-free baking powder

½ tsp fine sea salt

½ cup (60 g) unsalted pistachios, roughly chopped

½ cup (95 g) dried apricots, roughly chopped

½ cup (38 g) shredded coconut

2 large eggs, room temperature

1 cup (240 ml) unsweetened coconut milk, room temperature

⅓ cup (80 ml) avocado oil

2 tbsp (30 ml) fresh lemon juice (from 1 lemon)

2 tsp (10 ml) lemon extract

1 tsp pure vanilla extract

3–5 drops yellow food coloring, optional

I like to think of this as a modern take on a fruitcake, except it's actually edible. Like a traditional fruitcake, it contains dried fruit, nuts and lemon peel, but it isn't soaked in alcohol, it can't be kept at room temperature indefinitely and it doesn't weigh as much as a newborn baby. The brightness from the three different layers of lemon combined with coconut, apricots and pistachios are what make it feel fresh and modern. While the combo may sound strange, the flavors work really well together! It's a type of fruit cake that you'd truly love to eat. If you'd like a glaze with this bread, make the glaze from my Classic Lemon Bread with Lemon Glaze (page 84).

Preheat the oven to 350°F (177°C) and spray a 9 x 5–inch (23 x 13–cm) loaf pan with nonstick spray or coat with homemade pan release (page 180). Then line it with parchment paper and set aside.

Add the granulated sugar and lemon zest to a large bowl. Rub the zest into the sugar to help release the natural oils.

Add the gluten-free flour blend, xanthan gum, baking powder and salt. Whisk until they're all combined.

Whisk in the pistachios, apricots and coconut, then set aside.

In a medium bowl, whisk together the eggs, coconut milk, oil, lemon juice, lemon extract and vanilla extract. Whisk in the yellow food coloring, if using.

Pour the wet ingredients into the dry ingredients. Mix until they're just combined, then transfer the batter to the prepared baking pan.

Bake for 50 to 60 minutes or until a cake tester or toothpick inserted in the middle comes out clean. Cool it in the pan for 30 minutes, then remove the bread from the pan and cool it completely on a wire rack.

STORAGE NOTE: Keep the bread covered in an airtight container at room temperature for up to 3 days. To freeze, wrap tightly in plastic wrap, then freeze in a freezer-safe bag for up to 3 months.

LEMON BLUEBERRY BREAD

1 cup (195 g) granulated sugar

Zest from 1 lemon

2 cups (260 g) Sharon's Gluten-Free Flour Blend (page 179)

½ tsp xanthan gum

2 tsp (7 g) aluminum-free baking powder

½ tsp fine sea salt

2 large eggs, room temperature

1 cup (240 ml) unsweetened coconut milk, room temperature

⅓ cup (80 ml) avocado oil

1 tsp lemon extract

1 tsp pure vanilla extract

3–5 drops yellow food coloring, optional

1 cup (155 g) fresh blueberries

This bread is like summer in a loaf pan. Bright lemon paired with fresh blueberries is pure delight. I chose not to add a glaze to this bread, but if you're a big fan of glazed lemon breads, you can add the glaze from my Classic Lemon Bread with Lemon Glaze recipe (page 84). This bread is best with fresh blueberries. You could use frozen blueberries, but they will add a little bit more moisture to the bread and you will have to increase the baking time by 5 to 10 minutes.

Preheat the oven to 350°F (177°C) and spray a 9 x 5–inch (23 x 13–cm) loaf pan with nonstick spray or coat with homemade pan release (page 180), then line it with parchment paper.

Add the granulated sugar and lemon zest to a large bowl. Rub the zest into the sugar to help release the natural oils.

Add the gluten-free flour blend, xanthan gum, baking powder and salt. Whisk until they're combined and then set it aside.

In a medium bowl, whisk together the eggs, coconut milk, oil, lemon extract and vanilla extract. Whisk in the yellow food coloring, if using.

Pour the wet ingredients into the dry ingredients. Mix until just combined, then gently fold in the blueberries. Transfer the batter to the prepared baking pan.

Bake for 50 to 60 minutes or until a cake tester or toothpick inserted in the middle comes out clean. Cool it in the pan for 20 minutes, then remove the bread from the pan and cool it completely on a wire rack.

STORAGE NOTE: Store the bread wrapped tightly in plastic wrap at room temperature for up to 3 days. To freeze it, tightly wrap the whole loaf, sliced or unsliced, in plastic wrap and place it in a freezer-safe bag. Freeze for up to 3 months.

CHERRY LIME QUICK BREAD

1 cup (195 g) granulated sugar

1 tbsp (6 g) lime zest (from 2 small limes)

2 cups (260 g) Sharon's Gluten-Free Flour Blend (page 179)

1 tsp xanthan gum

1 tsp aluminum-free baking powder

½ tsp baking soda

½ tsp fine sea salt

2 large eggs, room temperature

1 cup (240 ml) unsweetened coconut milk, room temperature

⅓ cup (80 ml) avocado oil

1 tsp pure vanilla extract

2 tbsp (30 ml) fresh lime juice (from 2 small limes)

1 (10-oz [284-g]) jar maraschino cherries, drained, rinsed, dried and roughly chopped

The flavor of this bread reminds me of Cherry 7UP. It's got a sweet cherry taste with a subtle citrus flavor. When eating this bread, you first taste the sweetness of the maraschino cherries, and the lime comes through afterward. It's almost like that striped chewing gum from the '90s that changed flavor as you chewed, though not nearly as dramatic.

Preheat the oven to 350°F (177°C) and spray a 9 x 5–inch (23 x 13–cm) loaf pan with nonstick spray or coat with homemade pan release (page 180). Then line it with parchment paper and set aside.

In a large bowl, add the granulated sugar and lime zest. Use your fingers to rub the zest into the sugar to help release the natural oils.

Add the gluten-free flour blend, xanthan gum, baking powder, baking soda and salt. Whisk them together and set the mixture aside.

In a medium bowl, whisk together the eggs, coconut milk, oil, vanilla extract and lime juice.

Pour the wet ingredients into the dry ingredients. Mix until just combined, then fold in the cherries.

Transfer the batter to the prepared baking pan and bake for 50 to 60 minutes or until a cake tester or toothpick inserted in the middle comes out clean.

Cool it in the pan for 20 minutes, then remove the bread from the pan and parchment paper and allow it to cool completely on a wire rack.

STORAGE NOTE Store the bread wrapped tightly in plastic wrap at room temperature for up to 3 days. To freeze it, tightly wrap the whole loaf, sliced or unsliced, in plastic wrap and place it in a freezer-safe bag. Freeze for up to 3 months.

MEYER LEMON BREAD

FOR THE BREAD

1 cup (195 g) granulated sugar

Zest from 1 Meyer lemon

2 cups (260 g) Sharon's Gluten-Free Flour Blend (page 179)

½ tsp xanthan gum

1 tsp aluminum-free baking powder

½ tsp baking soda

½ tsp fine sea salt

2 large eggs, room temperature

¾ cup (180 ml) unsweetened coconut milk

2 tbsp (30 ml) fresh Meyer lemon juice

⅓ cup (80 ml) avocado oil

1 tsp pure vanilla extract

FOR THE GLAZE

1 cup (132 g) powdered sugar

Zest from 1 Meyer lemon

Juice from ½ Meyer lemon (about 1 tbsp [15 ml])

This is a favorite on my blog. It's full of bright, fresh citrus flavor but it's not as tart as a typical lemon loaf. Meyer lemons are a bit sweeter and less acidic than regular lemons, since they're thought to be a cross between regular lemons and Mandarin oranges. If you haven't tried Meyer lemons before, you're in for a real treat. If you ask me, I think they're a culinary delight—something fun and a little different without getting too crazy.

Preheat the oven to 350°F (177°C) and spray a 9 x 5–inch (23 x 13–cm) loaf pan with nonstick spray or coat with homemade pan release (page 180). Then line it with parchment paper and set it aside.

Add the granulated sugar and lemon zest to a large bowl. Rub the zest into the sugar to help release the natural oils.

Add the gluten-free flour blend, xanthan gum, baking powder, baking soda and salt. Whisk them until combined and then set the mixture aside.

In a medium bowl, whisk together the eggs, coconut milk, lemon juice, oil and vanilla extract.

Pour the wet ingredients into the dry ingredients. Mix until just combined, then transfer the batter to the prepared baking pan.

Bake for 50 to 60 minutes or until a cake tester or toothpick inserted into the middle comes out clean. Cool it in the pan for 30 minutes, then finish cooling completely on a wire rack before adding the glaze.

To make the glaze, add the powdered sugar, lemon zest and lemon juice to a bowl. Stir until it is smooth and thin enough to drizzle. If the glaze is too thick after adding the lemon juice, add 1 teaspoon of unsweetened coconut milk at a time until it's thin enough to drizzle.

STORAGE NOTES: Keep the bread covered in an airtight container at room temperature for up to 3 days. To freeze the glazed bread, slice into individual pieces, then freeze flat on a sheet pan. Then transfer the frozen slices to a freezer-safe bag and place wax paper between each piece. Defrost at room temperature.

To freeze the bread without glaze, wrap tightly in plastic wrap, then freeze in a freezer-safe bag for up to 3 months.

ORANGE DREAMSICLE BREAD

FOR THE FILLING

4 oz (113 g) dairy-free cream cheese, room temperature

1 large egg, room temperature

⅓ cup (65 g) granulated sugar

¼ cup (33 g) Sharon's Gluten-Free Flour Blend (page 179)

1 tsp pure vanilla extract

FOR THE BREAD

2 cups (260 g) Sharon's Gluten-Free Flour Blend (page 179)

1 tsp xanthan gum

1 tsp aluminum-free baking powder

½ tsp baking soda

½ tsp fine sea salt

1 cup (195 g) granulated sugar

2 large eggs, room temperature

⅔ cup (160 ml) unsweetened coconut milk, room temperature

⅓ cup (80 ml) pulp-free orange juice

⅓ cup (80 ml) avocado oil

1½ tsp (7 ml) orange extract

Orange food coloring, optional

STORAGE NOTE:

Store the bread wrapped tightly in plastic wrap at room temperature for up to 3 days. To freeze it, tightly wrap the whole loaf, sliced or unsliced, in plastic wrap and place it in a freezer-safe bag. Freeze for up to 3 months.

This bread is my baked version of another popular frozen treat. Layers of orange and vanilla taste just as bright and delicious in the form of a baked good! I thought about adding orange zest to this recipe, like I did with my Orange Poppy Seed Bread (page 100), but I thought that extra step would make it a little too "fancy" and a far reach from its humble beginning as an ice cream truck staple. Instead, this bread gets its flavor from orange juice (I use pulp-free) and orange extract. For a more intense orange flavor, use an additional ½ teaspoon of orange extract. I also used a little orange food coloring to give it that classic look. You can use a natural orange food coloring, or skip it completely if you prefer.

Preheat the oven to 350°F (177°C) and spray a 9 x 5–inch (23 x 13–cm) loaf pan with nonstick spray or coat with homemade pan release (page 180). Then line it with parchment paper and set aside.

To make the filling, add the dairy-free cream cheese and the egg to a medium bowl. Use a hand mixer to beat them together until smooth and creamy, about 1 to 2 minutes. Add the granulated sugar, gluten-free flour blend and vanilla extract. Beat for another minute until smooth. Set this mixture aside.

To make the bread, in a large bowl, whisk together the gluten-free flour blend, xanthan gum, baking powder, baking soda, salt and granulated sugar. Set this aside.

In a medium bowl, whisk together the eggs, coconut milk, orange juice, oil, orange extract and orange food coloring, if using.

Pour the wet ingredients into the dry ingredients. Mix them until just combined.

Pour half of the batter into the prepared baking pan. Add the cream cheese filling on top, gently smoothing it out without pressing it into the batter. Top with the remaining batter, gently spreading it evenly in the pan.

Bake for 50 to 60 minutes or until done. Be careful not to over-bake this one–the cream cheese filling will make your toothpick come out a little gooey. Mine was done after 55 minutes of baking.

Cool it in the pan for 20 minutes, then remove the bread from the pan and parchment paper and allow it to cool on a wire rack.

ORANGE POPPY SEED BREAD

FOR THE BREAD

1 cup (195 g) granulated sugar

Zest from 1 navel orange

2 cups (260 g) Sharon's Gluten-Free Flour Blend (page 179)

1 tsp xanthan gum

1 tsp aluminum-free baking powder

½ tsp baking soda

½ tsp fine sea salt

2 tbsp (19 g) poppy seeds

2 large eggs, room temperature

1 cup (240 ml) unsweetened coconut milk, room temperature

⅓ cup (80 ml) avocado oil

1 tsp orange extract

3–5 drops orange food coloring, optional

FOR THE GLAZE

1 cup (132 g) powdered sugar

Zest from ½ navel orange

1–2 tbsp (15–30 ml) fresh orange juice

This is a twist on the popular lemon poppy seed bread. It gets its flavor from orange zest and orange extract. Taking the extra step of rubbing the zest into the sugar really helps bring out the orange essence, releasing the natural oils in the zest to make the flavor more pronounced. You can add an additional ½ teaspoon of orange extract if you like a stronger orange taste.

Preheat the oven to 350°F (177°C) and spray a 9 x 5–inch (23 x 13–cm) loaf pan with nonstick spray or coat with homemade pan release (page 180). Then line it with parchment paper and set the pan aside.

Add the granulated sugar and orange zest to a large bowl. Rub the zest into the sugar to help release the natural oils.

Add the gluten-free flour blend, xanthan gum, baking powder, baking soda, salt and poppy seeds. Whisk them together and set the mixture aside.

In a medium bowl, whisk together the eggs, coconut milk, oil, orange extract and orange food coloring (if using).

Pour the wet ingredients into the dry ingredients. Mix them until they're just combined, then transfer the batter to the prepared baking pan.

Bake for 50 to 60 minutes or until done, being careful not to over-bake. Cool the bread in the pan for 20 minutes, then remove the bread from the pan and parchment paper and cool completely on a wire rack before adding the glaze.

To make the glaze, add the powdered sugar, orange zest and orange juice to a bowl. Stir them together until they are smooth and thin enough to drizzle. If the glaze is too thick after adding the orange juice, add 1 teaspoon of unsweetened coconut milk at a time until it's thin enough to drizzle.

STORAGE NOTES: Keep the bread covered in an airtight container at room temperature for up to 3 days. To freeze the glazed bread, slice into individual pieces, then freeze flat on a sheet pan. Then transfer the frozen slices to a freezer-safe bag and place wax paper between each piece. Defrost at room temperature.

To freeze the bread without glaze, wrap tightly in plastic wrap, then freeze in a freezer-safe bag for up to 3 months.

LEMON CRUMB BREAD

This is a cross between my Classic Lemon Bread with Lemon Glaze (page 84) and my Coffee Cake Quick Bread (page 166). Like the classic lemon bread, it's flavored with lemon in three different ways, and it's got an extra dose of lemon zest in the crumb topping as well. It's important to use fresh lemon juice here; do not use concentrated from the bottle. I've also added a little butter extract to give the bread more of a classic coffee cake flavor. If you really want to make this bread extra special, make half of the lemon glaze (page 84) and schmear it over the bread before serving.

FOR THE CRUMB TOPPING

¾ cup (100 g) Sharon's Gluten-Free Flour Blend (page 179)

¼ cup (55 g) light brown sugar, packed

¼ tsp xanthan gum

Zest from 1 lemon

¼ cup (55 g) refined coconut oil, measured solid then melted

FOR THE BREAD

⅔ cup (130 g) granulated sugar

Zest from 1 lemon

2 cups (260 g) Sharon's Gluten-Free Flour Blend (page 179)

¼ tsp xanthan gum

1½ tsp (7 g) aluminum-free baking powder

¼ tsp baking soda

½ tsp fine sea salt

2 large eggs, room temperature

⅔ cup (160 ml) unsweetened coconut milk, room temperature

⅓ cup (80 ml) avocado oil

2 tbsp (30 ml) fresh lemon juice

2 tsp (10 ml) lemon extract

1 tsp butter extract

3–5 drops yellow food coloring, optional

Preheat the oven to 350°F (177°C) and spray a 9 x 5–inch (23 x 13–cm) loaf pan with nonstick spray or coat with homemade pan release (page 180). Then line with parchment paper and set aside.

To make the crumb topping, add the gluten-free flour blend, brown sugar, xanthan gum and lemon zest to a bowl and stir to combine. Stir in the melted coconut oil until crumbs form. Set this mixture aside.

To make the bread, add the granulated sugar and lemon zest to a large bowl. Rub the zest into the sugar to help release the natural oils. Add the gluten-free flour blend, xanthan gum, baking powder, baking soda and salt. Whisk until combined and then set it aside.

In a medium bowl, whisk together the eggs, coconut milk, oil, lemon juice, lemon extract and butter extract. Whisk in the yellow food coloring, if using.

Pour the wet ingredients into the dry ingredients. Mix until they're just combined, then let the batter rest for 2 to 5 minutes to allow it to thicken.

Pour half of the batter into the prepared pan. Next, top with half of the crumb topping. Add the remaining batter to the pan and then top with the rest of the crumb topping.

Bake for 50 to 60 minutes or until a cake tester or toothpick inserted in the middle comes out clean. Cool it in the pan for 20 minutes, then remove the bread from the pan and parchment paper and cool it completely on a wire rack.

STORAGE NOTE: Store the bread wrapped tightly in plastic wrap at room temperature for up to 3 days. To freeze it, tightly wrap the whole loaf, sliced or unsliced, in plastic wrap and place it in a freezer-safe bag. Freeze for up to 3 months.

LEMON ZUCCHINI BREAD

1 cup (195 g) granulated sugar

Zest from 1 medium lemon

2 cups (260 g) Sharon's Gluten-Free Flour Blend (page 179)

¼ tsp xanthan gum

2 tsp (7 g) aluminum-free baking powder

½ tsp fine sea salt

2 large eggs, room temperature

¾ cup (180 ml) unsweetened coconut milk, room temperature

⅓ cup (80 ml) avocado oil

2 tbsp (30 ml) fresh lemon juice

1 tsp lemon extract

5–8 drops yellow food coloring, optional

1 cup (100 g) grated zucchini

Lemon juice and lemon zest make this bread light and fresh. It's a completely different experience and taste sensation from traditional zucchini bread (page 152) since it doesn't include the typical warm spices you'd expect. The combination of acid from the fresh lemon and the moisture from the zucchini gives this bread a nice, firm texture that holds up well for traveling. If you'd like a glaze with this bread, top with the lemon glaze from my Classic Lemon Bread with Lemon Glaze (page 84). This makes a great summertime bread to be enjoyed at breakfast, on picnics or as an afternoon snack.

Preheat the oven to 350°F (177°C) and spray a 9 x 5–inch (23 x 13–cm) loaf pan with nonstick spray or coat it with homemade pan release (page 180). Then line it with parchment paper and set aside.

Add the granulated sugar and lemon zest to a large bowl. Rub the zest into the sugar to help release the natural oils.

Add the gluten-free flour blend, xanthan gum, baking powder and salt. Whisk them until combined and then set this mixture aside.

In a medium bowl, whisk together the eggs, coconut milk, oil, lemon juice and lemon extract. Whisk in the yellow food coloring, if using.

Pour the wet ingredients into the dry ingredients. Mix them until just combined, then fold in the zucchini. Transfer the batter to the prepared baking pan.

Bake for 50 to 60 minutes or until a cake tester or toothpick inserted in the middle comes out clean. Cool it in the pan for 30 minutes, then remove the bread from the pan and cool it completely on a wire rack.

STORAGE NOTE: Store the bread wrapped tightly in plastic wrap at room temperature for up to 3 days. To freeze it, tightly wrap the whole loaf, sliced or unsliced, in plastic wrap and place it in a freezer-safe bag. Freeze for up to 3 months.

CHOCK FULL
O' AWESOME

SIMPLE FRUIT AND NUT BREADS

The quick breads in this chapter are bursting with nuts and fresh or dried fruit. They're hearty and full of flavor combinations I love while still being simple and easy to make—and best of all, they're gluten- and dairy-free, so you can feel good eating them! Some breads feature rich warm spices, like the dash of cinnamon in the Blackberry Peach Bread (page 112), while others make fresh produce or dried fruit shine, like the Sweet and Simple Raspberry Quick Bread (page 115). There's also the Cherry Oatmeal Bread (page 128), which is the perfect blank canvas recipe. You can change up the flavors and fruit based on what's in season or what your preferences are. One of my personal favorites is the Pistachio Bread (page 108). Unlike the pistachio bread you'd find at the grocery store, my version actually has pistachios in it—imagine that!

PISTACHIO BREAD

2 cups (260 g) Sharon's Gluten-Free Flour Blend (page 179)

1 tsp xanthan gum

1 tsp aluminum-free baking powder

½ tsp baking soda

½ tsp fine sea salt

1 cup (195 g) granulated sugar

½ cup (60 g) raw unsalted and shelled pistachios, chopped, plus 1 tbsp (8 g) for topping (optional)

2 large eggs, room temperature

1 cup (240 ml) unsweetened coconut milk, room temperature

⅓ cup plus 1 tbsp (95 ml) avocado oil

1½ tsp (7 ml) almond extract

5 drops green food coloring, optional

When I first bought a pistachio bread at the grocery store bakery, it brought back memories of the pistachio muffins I sold at my first job in a coffee shop. I loved the flavor and color of those muffins, so I had high hopes for the bread version. To my surprise, the "pistachio" bread had NO pistachios in it. My husband dubbed it "faux-stachio" bread, and the name has stuck. I recreated a gluten-free and dairy-free version of the bakery classic here, but my version also includes real pistachios. I probably should have called this "No Faux-stachio Bread" just for fun.

Preheat the oven to 350°F (177°C) and spray a 9 x 5–inch (23 x 13–cm) loaf pan with nonstick spray or coat with homemade pan release (page 180). Then line with parchment paper and set aside.

In a large bowl, whisk together the gluten-free flour blend, xanthan gum, baking powder, baking soda, salt and granulated sugar. Stir in ½ cup (60 g) chopped pistachios and set this aside.

In a medium bowl, whisk together the eggs, coconut milk, oil, almond extract and green food coloring, if using.

Pour the wet ingredients into the dry ingredients. Mix them until just combined, then transfer the batter to the prepared baking pan. Sprinkle the top with an additional 1 tablespoon (8 g) of chopped pistachios, if desired.

Bake for 50 to 60 minutes or until a cake tester or toothpick inserted in the middle comes out clean. Cool it in the pan for 20 minutes, then remove the bread from the pan and allow it to cool on a wire rack.

STORAGE NOTE: Store the bread wrapped tightly in plastic wrap at room temperature for up to 3 days. To freeze it, tightly wrap the whole loaf, sliced or unsliced, in plastic wrap and place it in a freezer-safe bag. Freeze for up to 3 months.

BLUEBERRY MUFFIN BREAD

2 cups (260 g) Sharon's Gluten-Free Flour Blend (page 179)

1 tsp xanthan gum

2 tsp (7 g) aluminum-free baking powder

½ tsp fine sea salt

1 tsp ground cinnamon

½ cup (97 g) granulated sugar

1½ cups (220 g) fresh blueberries

2 large eggs, room temperature

⅔ cup (160 ml) unsweetened coconut milk, room temperature

¼ cup (55 g) light brown sugar

⅓ cup (80 ml) avocado oil

1 tsp vanilla extract

1 tsp raw sugar, optional

This bread is based on—you guessed it—my blueberry muffin recipe! With a few tweaks, my favorite muffin recipe has been transformed into a gorgeous loaf bursting with fresh blueberries. It's got an amazing warm spice flavor from the ground cinnamon.

Cinnamon and blueberries just pair so beautifully together—I could have that flavor combo every day and never get sick of it. To keep this true to its muffin roots, sprinkle the top of the bread with some cinnamon sugar or raw sugar for a sweet little crunch.

Preheat the oven to 350°F (177°C) and spray a 9 x 5–inch (23 x 13–cm) loaf pan with nonstick spray or coat with homemade pan release (page 108). Then line it with parchment paper and set aside.

In a large bowl, whisk together the gluten-free flour blend, xanthan gum, baking powder, salt, cinnamon and granulated sugar. Gently stir in the fresh blueberries, then set this aside.

In a medium bowl, whisk together the eggs, coconut milk, brown sugar, oil and vanilla extract.

Pour the wet ingredients into the dry ingredients. Mix until just combined, then transfer the batter to the prepared baking pan. Sprinkle the top of the bread with the raw sugar, if you're using it.

Bake for 55 to 65 minutes or until a cake tester or toothpick inserted in the middle comes out clean. Cool it in the pan for 20 minutes, then remove the bread from the pan and cool on a wire rack.

STORAGE NOTE: Store the bread wrapped tightly in plastic wrap at room temperature for up to 3 days. To freeze it, tightly wrap the whole loaf, sliced or unsliced, in plastic wrap and place it in a freezer-safe bag. Freeze for up to 3 months.

BLACKBERRY PEACH BREAD

2 cups (260 g) Sharon's Gluten-Free Flour Blend (page 179)

1 tsp xanthan gum

½ cup (97 g) granulated sugar

1 tsp aluminum-free baking powder

½ tsp baking soda

½ tsp fine sea salt

1 tsp ground cinnamon

2 large eggs, room temperature

½ cup (112 g) light brown sugar, packed

⅔ cup (160 ml) unsweetened coconut milk, room temperature

⅓ cup (80 ml) avocado oil

1 tsp pure vanilla extract

¾ cup (115 g) fresh blackberries

½ cup (76 g) diced peaches

This bread features one of my favorite flavors of summer—fresh peaches. There's just nothing like a juicy, ripe peach. When they're really ripe, they tend to peel very easily by hand. You don't have to peel them before dicing them up to add to the batter, but I prefer them peeled.

If you want to make this out of season with canned diced peaches, be sure to drain them well before mixing them in. The blackberry + peach + cinnamon combo is one you must try; it's a delicious flavor sensation that'll make your taste buds dance.

Preheat the oven to 350°F (177°C) and spray a 9 x 5–inch (23 x 13–cm) loaf pan with nonstick spray or coat with homemade pan release (page 180), then line it with parchment paper.

In a large bowl, whisk together the gluten-free flour blend, xanthan gum, granulated sugar, baking powder, baking soda, salt and cinnamon. Set this mixture aside.

In a medium bowl, whisk together the eggs, brown sugar, coconut milk, oil and vanilla extract.

Pour the wet ingredients into the dry ingredients. Mix them until just combined, then gently fold in the blackberries and peaches. Transfer the batter to the prepared baking pan, spreading it evenly in the pan.

Bake for 50 to 60 minutes or until a cake tester or toothpick inserted in the middle comes out clean. Cool this bread in the pan for 20 minutes, then remove the bread from the pan, remove the parchment paper and allow it to cool on a wire rack.

STORAGE NOTE: Store the bread wrapped tightly in plastic wrap at room temperature for up to 3 days. To freeze it, tightly wrap the whole loaf, sliced or unsliced, in plastic wrap and place it in a freezer-safe bag. Freeze for up to 3 months.

SWEET AND SIMPLE RASPBERRY QUICK BREAD

2 cups (260 g) Sharon's Gluten-Free Flour Blend (page 179)

1 tsp xanthan gum

1 cup (195 g) granulated sugar

2 tsp (7 g) aluminum-free baking powder

¼ tsp baking soda

½ tsp fine sea salt

1 pint (310 g) fresh raspberries

2 large eggs, room temperature

⅔ cup (160 ml) unsweetened coconut milk, room temperature

⅓ cup (80 ml) avocado oil

2 tsp (10 ml) white vinegar

1 tsp pure vanilla extract

This bread is an updated recipe from my blog. It was one of my first bread recipes and needed quite a bit of reworking. This version is now dairy-free and has more moisture and a lighter texture. Essentially, it's no longer the same recipe—and for the better! I've also added more raspberries, because you can never go wrong with a little extra fresh fruit.

Preheat the oven to 350°F (177°C) and spray a 9 x 5–inch (23 x 13–cm) loaf pan with nonstick spray or coat with homemade pan release (page 180), then line it with parchment paper.

In a large bowl, whisk together the gluten-free flour blend, xanthan gum, granulated sugar, baking powder, baking soda and salt. Remove 1 tablespoon (8 g) of the flour mixture and gently toss it with the raspberries in a small bowl (being careful not to crush them) and set this aside.

In a medium bowl, whisk together the eggs, coconut milk, oil, vinegar and vanilla extract.

Pour the wet ingredients into the dry ingredients. Mix until they are just combined, then gently fold in the raspberries.

Transfer the batter to the prepared baking pan.

Bake for 50 to 60 minutes or until a cake tester or toothpick inserted in the middle comes out clean. Cool it in the pan for 20 minutes, then remove the bread from the pan, remove the parchment paper and cool on a wire rack.

STORAGE NOTE: Store the bread wrapped tightly in plastic wrap at room temperature for up to 3 days. To freeze it, tightly wrap the whole loaf, sliced or unsliced, in plastic wrap and place it in a freezer-safe bag. Freeze for up to 3 months.

MORNING GLORY QUICK BREAD

2 cups (260 g) Sharon's Gluten-Free Flour Blend (page 179)

1 tsp xanthan gum

1 tsp aluminum-free baking powder

½ tsp baking soda

½ tsp fine sea salt

2 tsp (5 g) ground cinnamon

⅓ cup (39 g) chopped walnuts

¼ cup (25 g) shredded coconut

2 large eggs, room temperature

⅔ cup (149 g) light brown sugar, packed

½ cup (120 ml) unsweetened coconut milk, room temperature

⅓ cup (80 ml) avocado oil

1 tsp pure vanilla extract

⅓ cup (51 g) raisins

½ cup (55 g) grated carrot

½ cup (47 g) grated Granny Smith apple

Morning Glory muffins are one of those classic recipes that everyone knows of, but they aren't super popular. They're loaded with nuts, fruit and even a little bit of veggies! The taste is similar to carrot cake, but healthier and more acceptable to eat for breakfast. Here, I've given the classic muffin a quick bread makeover. This recipe would also be great as mini loaves, just reduce the baking time to about 35 to 40 minutes. If you find that your raisins are dried out, put them in a bowl and cover them with hot water for about 5 minutes. It'll plump them right up! Just be sure to drain the water before adding them to the batter.

Preheat the oven to 350°F (177°C) and spray a 9 x 5–inch (23 x 13–cm) loaf pan with nonstick spray or coat with homemade pan release (page 180), then line it with parchment paper.

In a large bowl, whisk together the gluten-free flour blend, xanthan gum, baking powder, baking soda, salt and cinnamon. Stir in the walnuts and coconut, then set the mixture aside.

In a medium bowl, whisk together the eggs, brown sugar, coconut milk, oil and vanilla extract.

Pour the wet ingredients into the dry ingredients. Mix them until just combined, then fold in the raisins, carrot and apple.

Transfer the batter to the prepared baking pan. Bake for 50 to 60 minutes or until a cake tester or toothpick inserted in the middle comes out clean.

Cool it in the pan for 20 minutes, then remove the bread from the pan, remove the parchment paper and allow to cool completely on a wire rack.

STORAGE NOTE: Store the bread wrapped tightly in plastic wrap at room temperature for up to 3 days. To freeze it, tightly wrap the whole loaf, sliced or unsliced, in plastic wrap and place it in a freezer-safe bag. Freeze for up to 3 months.

BLUEBERRY PECAN QUICK BREAD

2 cups (260 g) Sharon's Gluten-Free Flour Blend (page 179)

1 tsp xanthan gum

1 tsp aluminum-free baking powder

½ tsp baking soda

½ tsp fine sea salt

1 cup (155 g) fresh blueberries

½ cup (60 g) chopped pecans

2 large eggs, room temperature

1 cup (223 g) light brown sugar, packed

1 cup (240 ml) unsweetened coconut milk, room temperature

⅓ cup (80 ml) avocado oil

1 tbsp (15 ml) white vinegar

2 tsp (10 ml) pure vanilla extract

This is a great, easy loaf to make when you've got some fresh blueberries on hand. I like to stir the blueberries and chopped pecans into the flour mixture. Alternatively, you can stir the blueberries and pecans together with 1 tablespoon (8 g) of the flour mixture and then fold it in at the end. Coating the fruit and nuts with flour helps keep them from sinking to the bottom of the bread while baking. I prefer taking the shortcut—it's one less bowl and a couple less steps without sacrificing flavor or texture.

Preheat the oven to 350°F (177°C) and spray a 9 x 5–inch (23 x 13–cm) loaf pan with nonstick spray or coat with homemade pan release (page 180), then line it with parchment paper.

In a large bowl, whisk together the gluten-free flour blend, xanthan gum, baking powder, baking soda and salt. Next, gently stir in the blueberries and pecans. Set the mixture aside.

In a medium bowl, whisk together the eggs, brown sugar, coconut milk, oil, vinegar and vanilla extract.

Pour the wet ingredients into the dry ingredients. Mix until they're just combined, then transfer the batter to the prepared baking pan.

Bake for 50 to 60 minutes or until a cake tester or toothpick inserted in the middle comes out clean. Cool it in the pan for 20 minutes, then remove the bread from the pan, remove the parchment paper and allow it to cool on a wire rack.

STORAGE NOTE: Store the bread wrapped tightly in plastic wrap at room temperature for up to 3 days. To freeze it, tightly wrap the whole loaf, sliced or unsliced, in plastic wrap and place it in a freezer-safe bag. Freeze for up to 3 months.

TRAIL MIX QUICK BREAD

2 cups (260 g) Sharon's Gluten-Free Flour Blend (page 179)

1 tsp xanthan gum

1 tsp aluminum-free baking powder

½ tsp baking soda

½ tsp fine sea salt

½ cup (97 g) granulated sugar

⅓ cup (67 g) dairy-free chocolate chips or chunks

⅓ cup (51 g) raisins

⅓ cup (45 g) unsalted roasted peanuts, roughly chopped

2 large eggs, room temperature

1 cup (240 ml) unsweetened coconut milk, room temperature

½ cup (112 g) light brown sugar, packed

⅓ cup (80 ml) avocado oil

1 tsp pure vanilla extract

The classic trail mix combo includes chocolate candy (usually M&Ms, but they're not dairy-free), peanuts and raisins. If you can find a dairy-free M&M-type candy, feel free to use that in place of the chocolate chips or chocolate chunks. The mix-ins here are really versatile. Feel free to switch up the fruits and nuts to make your own custom trail mix blend. If you're not a fan of raisins, you can swap them with your favorite dried fruit like cranberries or cherries. If you have a favorite pre-made trail mix, you can use that here, too! Just use 1 cup (150 g) of it to replace the chocolate, peanuts and raisins called for in this recipe.

Preheat the oven to 350°F (177°C) and spray a 9 x 5–inch (23 x 13–cm) loaf pan with nonstick spray or coat with homemade pan release (page 180). Then line it with parchment paper and set aside.

In a large bowl, whisk together the gluten-free flour blend, xanthan gum, baking powder, baking soda, salt and granulated sugar. Stir in the chocolate chips/chunks, raisins and peanuts. Set the mixture aside.

In a medium bowl, whisk together the eggs, coconut milk, brown sugar, oil and vanilla extract.

Pour the wet ingredients into the dry ingredients. Mix them until just combined, then transfer the batter to the prepared baking pan.

Bake for 50 to 60 minutes or until a cake tester or toothpick inserted in the middle comes out clean. Cool it in the pan for 20 minutes, then remove the bread from the pan and parchment paper and cool on a wire rack.

STORAGE NOTE: Store the bread wrapped tightly in plastic wrap at room temperature for up to 3 days. To freeze it, tightly wrap the whole loaf, sliced or unsliced, in plastic wrap and place it in a freezer-safe bag. Freeze for up to 3 months.

PEANUT BUTTER BREAD

2 cups (260 g) Sharon's Gluten-Free Flour Blend (page 179)

1 tsp xanthan gum

1 tsp aluminum-free baking powder

½ tsp baking soda

½ tsp fine sea salt

½ cup (97 g) granulated sugar

2 large eggs, room temperature

½ cup (112 g) light brown sugar, packed

1 cup (240 ml) unsweetened coconut milk, room temperature

¼ cup (60 ml) avocado oil

1 tsp pure vanilla extract

½ cup (91 g) creamy peanut butter, plus more for topping (optional)

This is almost like a giant, soft peanut butter cookie baked in a loaf pan. It's got a wonderfully subtle peanut butter flavor. Spread some of your favorite jam on this and you've got yourself the ultimate peanut butter and jelly "sandwich." I use creamy peanut butter here, and you can use regular or no-stir natural peanut butter. If you need nut-free, try this bread with Wowbutter in place of the peanut butter. If you prefer almond butter, Barney's brand is the best option for this recipe. Flavor twist: add some chopped peanuts for crunch or some dairy-free chocolate chips for a peanut butter chocolate chip bread!

Preheat the oven to 350°F (177°C) and spray a 9 x 5–inch (23 x 13–cm) loaf pan with nonstick spray or coat with homemade pan release (page 180). Then line it with parchment paper and set aside.

In a large bowl, whisk together the gluten-free flour blend, xanthan gum, baking powder, baking soda, salt and granulated sugar. Set this mixture aside.

In a medium bowl, whisk together the eggs, brown sugar, coconut milk, oil and vanilla extract. Set this aside.

Melt the peanut butter in a microwave-safe bowl for 20 seconds until it's thin enough to pour. Whisk the peanut butter into the wet ingredients until incorporated.

Pour the dry ingredients into the wet ingredients. Mix until just combined, then transfer the batter to the prepared baking pan.

Bake for 50 to 60 minutes or until a cake tester or toothpick inserted in the middle comes out clean. Cool it in the pan for 20 minutes, then remove the bread from the pan and parchment paper and cool on a wire rack.

Drizzle the bread with additional melted peanut butter before serving if desired.

STORAGE NOTE: Store the bread wrapped tightly in plastic wrap at room temperature for up to 3 days. To freeze it, tightly wrap the whole loaf, sliced or unsliced, in plastic wrap and place it in a freezer-safe bag. Freeze for up to 3 months.

MAPLE WALNUT BREAD

2 cups (260 g) Sharon's Gluten-Free Flour Blend (page 179)

1 tsp xanthan gum

1 tsp aluminum-free baking powder

½ tsp baking soda

½ tsp fine sea salt

½ cup plus 1 tbsp (67 g) chopped walnuts, divided

2 large eggs, room temperature

½ cup (112 g) light brown sugar, packed

¾ cup (180 ml) walnut milk, room temperature

½ cup (120 ml) pure maple syrup

⅓ cup (80 ml) avocado oil

1 tsp pure vanilla extract

½ tsp maple extract

This bread gets its distinct maple flavor from pure maple syrup and maple extract. Maple and walnut is a classic New England flavor combination, and this bread will make you feel like you've just taken a trip to the sugar house. If you have maple sugar, use that in place of the brown sugar and omit the maple extract. If you can't find it, no sweat—this still has a great maple flavor. You can use unsweetened coconut milk beverage in place of the walnut milk. The walnut milk I get is slightly sweetened (it has about 4 grams of sugar per serving) and it adds an extra dimension of nuttiness to the bread.

. . . .

Preheat the oven to 350°F (177°C) and spray a 9 x 5–inch (23 x 13–cm) loaf pan with nonstick spray or coat with homemade pan release (page 180), then line it with parchment paper.

In a large bowl, whisk together the gluten-free flour blend, xanthan gum, baking powder, baking soda and salt. Stir in ½ cup (59 g) chopped walnuts and set this aside.

In a medium bowl, whisk together the eggs, brown sugar, walnut milk, maple syrup, oil, vanilla extract and maple extract.

Pour the wet ingredients into the dry ingredients. Mix until just combined, then transfer the batter to the prepared baking pan. Top the batter with the remaining 1 tablespoon (8 g) of chopped walnuts.

Bake for 50 to 60 minutes or until a cake tester or toothpick inserted in the middle comes out clean. Cool it in the pan for 20 minutes, then remove the bread from the pan, remove the parchment paper and cool the bread on a wire rack.

STORAGE NOTE: Store the bread wrapped tightly in plastic wrap at room temperature for up to 3 days. To freeze it, tightly wrap the whole loaf, sliced or unsliced, in plastic wrap and place it in a freezer-safe bag. Freeze for up to 3 months.

DATE NUT BREAD

¾ cup (88 g) chopped walnuts

1 cup (153 g) chopped dates

1½ tsp (7 g) baking soda

½ tsp fine sea salt

¼ cup (45 g) palm shortening

¾ cup (180 ml) boiling water

2 large eggs, room temperature

½ tsp pure vanilla extract

1 cup (195 g) granulated sugar

¾ tsp xanthan gum

1½ cups (195 g) Sharon's Gluten-Free Flour Blend (page 179)

This bread is from an old recipe given to my mom by her best friend's mother, Mrs. Purdy. My mom has made this bread every year at Thanksgiving, Christmas and Easter for as long as I can remember. It's one of her favorites. This bread has a very different mixing process (as many old-fashioned recipes seem to have) and yields a dense but tasty loaf.

Preheat the oven to 350°F (177°C) and spray a 9 x 5–inch (23 x 13–cm) loaf pan with nonstick spray or coat with homemade pan release (page 180). Then line it with parchment paper and set aside.

In a medium heat-proof bowl, combine the walnuts, dates, baking soda, salt, shortening and boiling water. Let sit for 15 minutes.

In a large bowl, whisk together the eggs, vanilla extract, sugar and xanthan gum.

Add the date/walnut mixture to the egg mixture once the 15 minutes has lapsed. Stir to combine, then stir in the gluten-free flour until it's completely moistened.

Bake for 55 to 60 minutes or until a cake tester or toothpick inserted in the middle comes out clean.

Cool it in the pan for 20 minutes, then remove the bread from the pan and parchment paper and allow to cool on a wire rack.

STORAGE NOTE: Store the bread wrapped tightly in plastic wrap at room temperature for up to 3 days. To freeze it, tightly wrap the whole loaf, sliced or unsliced, in plastic wrap and place it in a freezer-safe bag. Freeze for up to 3 months.

CHERRY OATMEAL BREAD

1½ cups (195 g) Sharon's Gluten-Free Flour Blend (page 179)

1 tsp xanthan gum

½ cup (60 g) gluten-free oat flour

¼ cup (39 g) gluten-free oats

¼ cup (49 g) granulated sugar

1 tsp aluminum-free baking powder

½ tsp baking soda

½ tsp fine sea salt

½ cup (60 g) chopped pecans

2 large eggs, room temperature

1 cup (240 ml) unsweetened coconut milk, room temperature

½ cup (123 g) dairy-free plain or vanilla yogurt

½ cup (112 g) light brown sugar, packed

⅓ cup (80 ml) avocado oil

1½ tsp (7 ml) pure vanilla extract

⅔ cup (90 g) fresh or frozen cherries, roughly chopped

Adding gluten-free oatmeal and gluten-free oats to this bread makes it hearty and great for breakfast or snacks. I use fresh cherries, but if you use frozen cherries, be sure to defrost them first and drain the excess liquid. You can also substitute blueberries if you prefer! This bread has a cherry-vanilla flavor profile, but feel free to add a little cinnamon or almond extract to change it up once in a while. You can even use an equal amount of vanilla bean paste in place of the vanilla extract. This is the only recipe in the book that calls for gluten-free oats and gluten-free oat flour—be sure to use purity protocol oats if you have Celiac Disease. You can also make your own oat flour by grinding your oats in a food processor or high-speed blender until they are a fine powder that resembles flour.

Preheat the oven to 350°F (177°C) and spray a 9 x 5–inch (23 x 13–cm) loaf pan with nonstick spray or coat with homemade pan release (page 180), then line it with parchment paper.

In a large bowl, whisk together the gluten-free flour blend, xanthan gum, gluten-free oat flour, gluten-free oats, sugar, baking powder, baking soda and salt. Whisk in the chopped pecans and set it aside.

In a medium bowl, whisk together the eggs, coconut milk, yogurt, brown sugar, oil and vanilla extract.

Pour the wet ingredients into the dry ingredients. Mix until they're just combined, then fold in the cherries. Transfer the batter to the prepared baking pan.

Bake for 55 to 65 minutes or until a cake tester or toothpick inserted in the middle comes out clean. Cool it in the pan for 20 minutes, then remove the bread from the pan, remove the parchment paper and allow to cool completely on a wire rack.

STORAGE NOTE: Store the bread wrapped tightly in plastic wrap at room temperature for up to 3 days. To freeze it, tightly wrap the whole loaf, sliced or unsliced, in plastic wrap and place it in a freezer-safe bag. Freeze for up to 3 months.

BAKING FOR ALL SEASONS

EASY HOLIDAY BREADS AND BREADS WITH SEASONAL PRODUCE

When the mood strikes for some seasonal baking, start with these quick breads! They feature prominent flavors for every time of year, and all of them come together quickly and with minimal work. When spring hits after a long winter, there are breads to make the most of whatever fresh seasonal produce is popping up in your garden, like the Strawberry Rhubarb Coffee Cake Bread (page 151). When the weather grows cooler, turn to the plethora of pumpkin breads filled with warm spices and fall flavors. And when the madness of the holidays descends, save your sanity with something like the Iced Gingerbread Loaf (page 144) which is perfect for gifting, or Champagne Bread (page 148) for some added festive flavor to your gluten-free, dairy-free brunch celebrations. Bake your way through the seasons and treat your taste buds to a year-round trip to Flavortown.

MAMA'S APPLE CINNAMON BREAD

2 cups (260 g) Sharon's Gluten-Free Flour Blend (page 179)

1 tsp xanthan gum

1 tsp baking powder

½ tsp baking soda

½ tsp fine sea salt

2 tsp (5 g) ground cinnamon

¼ tsp ground nutmeg

⅛ tsp allspice

½ cup (97 g) granulated sugar

½ cup (59 g) chopped walnuts

2 large eggs, room temperature

⅔ cup (160 ml) apple cider, room temperature

½ cup (112 g) light brown sugar

⅓ cup (80 ml) avocado oil

1 tsp pure vanilla extract

1 medium Braeburn apple, finely diced

This is my grandmother's "recipe"—one that she makes so frequently she doesn't actually have a recipe for it. She told me all of the ingredients she uses to make the bread, so I went to work turning a list of ingredients into measurable amounts. I think I did pretty well! This bread is actually one of my favorites in the entire cookbook. I love the combination of the apples and spices; it's such a comforting bread full of fall flavor. My husband rated this a 10 (out of 10), which he almost never does when there isn't any chocolate involved. This one is a real winner in both taste and sentiment.

Preheat the oven to 350°F (177°C) and spray a 9 x 5–inch (23 x 13–cm) loaf pan with nonstick spray or coat with homemade pan release (page 180), then line it with parchment paper.

In a large bowl, whisk together the gluten-free flour blend, xanthan gum, baking powder, baking soda, salt, cinnamon, nutmeg, allspice and granulated sugar. Stir in the walnuts and set it aside.

In a medium bowl, whisk together the eggs, apple cider, brown sugar, oil and vanilla extract.

Pour the wet ingredients into the dry ingredients. Mix them until just combined. Add the diced apples; gently fold them into the batter, then transfer the batter to the prepared baking pan.

Bake for 55 to 65 minutes or until a cake tester or toothpick inserted in the middle comes out clean. Cool in the pan for 30 minutes, then remove the bread from the pan and cool completely on a wire rack.

STORAGE NOTE: Store the bread wrapped tightly in plastic wrap at room temperature for up to 3 days. To freeze it, tightly wrap the whole loaf, sliced or unsliced, in plastic wrap and place it in a freezer-safe bag. Freeze for up to 3 months.

PUMPKIN COCONUT QUICK BREAD

2 cups (260 g) Sharon's Gluten-Free Flour Blend (page 179)

1 tsp xanthan gum

½ cup (97 g) granulated sugar

2 tsp (3 g) Homemade Pumpkin Pie Spice (page 179)

1 tsp aluminum-free baking powder

½ tsp baking soda

½ tsp fine sea salt

½ cup (38 g) shredded coconut

2 large eggs, room temperature

1 cup (270 g) pumpkin puree

½ cup (112 g) light brown sugar

⅔ cup (160 ml) unsweetened coconut milk

⅓ cup (74 g) coconut oil, measured solid then melted

1 tsp pure vanilla extract

½ tsp coconut extract

1 tbsp (7 g) flaked coconut

Summer meets fall with this tropical twist on a fall-favorite bread! This has all the pleasant flavors of pumpkin spice and is sprinkled with shredded coconut. You could even use an additional teaspoon of pumpkin pie spice if you prefer a stronger spice flavor. It's perfect for late summer when you're set for fall but you're not quite ready to give up on summer. It's the best of both seasons, all in one bite.

Preheat the oven to 350°F (177°C) and spray a 9 x 5–inch (23 x 13–cm) loaf pan with nonstick spray or coat with homemade pan release (page 180), then line it with a piece of parchment paper, leaving enough of an overhang to pull the bread out of the pan.

In a large bowl, whisk together the gluten-free flour blend, xanthan gum, granulated sugar, pumpkin pie spice, baking powder, baking soda and salt. Stir in the shredded coconut and set it aside.

In a medium bowl, whisk together the eggs, pumpkin puree, brown sugar, coconut milk, melted coconut oil, vanilla extract and coconut extract.

Pour the wet ingredients into the dry ingredients and stir until combined.

Transfer the batter to the prepared loaf pan, spreading it evenly. Top it with the coconut flakes.

Bake for 50 to 65 minutes or until a tester inserted in the middle comes out clean. Cool it in the pan for 20 minutes, then use the parchment paper to lift the bread out of the pan and cool on a wire rack (removing the parchment paper). Cool completely before slicing.

STORAGE NOTE: Store the bread wrapped tightly in plastic wrap at room temperature for up to 3 days. To freeze it, tightly wrap the whole loaf, sliced or unsliced, in plastic wrap and place it in a freezer-safe bag. Freeze for up to 3 months.

SWEET POTATO BREAD

2 cups (260 g) Sharon's Gluten-Free Flour Blend (page 179)

¾ tsp xanthan gum

1 tsp aluminum-free baking powder

½ tsp baking soda

½ tsp fine sea salt

1 tsp ground cinnamon

½ tsp ground nutmeg

½ cup (60 g) chopped pecans, plus 1–2 tbsp (8–15 g) for topping (optional)

1 cup (211 g) mashed sweet potato

2 large eggs, room temperature

¾ cup (168 g) light brown sugar

⅔ cup (160 ml) unsweetened coconut milk

2 tsp (10 ml) white vinegar

⅓ cup (80 ml) avocado oil

1 tsp pure vanilla extract

This is a great fall or winter quick bread when sweet potatoes are plentiful. I've made this with leftover mashed sweet potatoes that were doctored with butter and cream for holiday meals, leftover sweet potato casserole that had a pecan topping (minus the marshmallows) and with plain, regular old mashed sweet potatoes I made specifically to use with this recipe. It's great to know that you can basically use any type of mashed sweet potato here, but if you use leftover sweet potato casserole that has a marshmallow topping, scrape that off before measuring your cup. The marshmallow will melt when it bakes, leaving you less than a cup (211 g) of sweet potato, and may cause unpleasant sticky/chewy spots in the bread. I love eating this bread with a thin little schmear of dairy-free cream cheese.

Preheat the oven to 350°F (177°C) and spray a 9 x 5–inch (23 x 13–cm) loaf pan with nonstick spray or coat with homemade pan release (page 180), then line it with parchment paper.

In a large bowl, whisk together the gluten-free flour blend, xanthan gum, baking powder, baking soda, salt, cinnamon and nutmeg. Stir in the chopped pecans and set this aside.

In a medium bowl, whisk together the mashed sweet potato, eggs, brown sugar, coconut milk, vinegar, oil and vanilla extract.

Pour the wet ingredients into the dry ingredients and stir them until combined.

Transfer the batter to the prepared loaf pan, spreading it evenly. Sprinkle the top of the bread with 1 to 2 tablespoons (8 to 15 g) of additional chopped pecans if desired.

Bake for 50 to 60 minutes or until a tester inserted in the middle comes out clean.

Cool it in the pan for 20 minutes, then remove from the pan and parchment paper and cool completely on a wire rack.

STORAGE NOTE: Store the bread wrapped tightly in plastic wrap at room temperature for up to 3 days. To freeze it, tightly wrap the whole loaf, sliced or unsliced, in plastic wrap and place it in a freezer-safe bag. Freeze for up to 3 months.

CLASSIC(ISH) CRANBERRY BREAD

2 cups (260 g) Sharon's Gluten-Free Flour Blend (page 179)

1 tsp xanthan gum

1 tsp aluminum-free baking powder

½ tsp baking soda

½ tsp fine sea salt

½ tsp ground cinnamon

½ cup (59 g) chopped walnuts or pecans

2 large eggs, room temperature

1 cup (223 g) light brown sugar, packed

⅔ cup (160 ml) unsweetened coconut milk, room temperature

⅓ cup (80 ml) orange juice, pulp-free

⅓ cup (80 ml) avocado oil

1 tsp pure vanilla extract

1½ cups (165 g) fresh cranberries, roughly chopped

The classic cranberry bread you see all over the internet is more of a cranberry orange bread and is made with quite a bit of orange juice and zest. Since I already have a cranberry orange bread on my blog, I wanted to make it a little different. While I do use a little bit of orange juice because the orange complements the cranberry flavor, I also added a little bit of cinnamon. For even more depth of flavor, toast your nuts in a dry pan for a few minutes until they're fragrant, then cool to room temperature before adding. After you make this bread, use the leftover cranberries to make Cranberry Swirl Bread (page 147).

Preheat the oven to 350°F (177°C) and spray a 9 x 5–inch (23 x 13–cm) loaf pan with nonstick spray or coat with homemade pan release (page 180). Then line it with parchment paper and set aside.

In a large bowl, whisk together the gluten-free flour blend, xanthan gum, baking powder, baking soda, salt and cinnamon. Whisk in the chopped nuts and set this mixture aside.

In a medium bowl, whisk together the eggs, brown sugar, coconut milk, orange juice, oil and vanilla extract.

Pour the wet ingredients into the dry ingredients and mix until they're just combined. Fold in the chopped cranberries, then transfer the batter to the prepared baking pan.

Bake for 50 to 60 minutes or until a cake tester or toothpick inserted in the middle comes out clean. Cool it in the pan for 20 minutes, then remove the bread from the pan and parchment paper and allow to completely cool on a wire rack.

STORAGE NOTE: Store the bread wrapped tightly in plastic wrap at room temperature for up to 3 days. To freeze it, tightly wrap the whole loaf, sliced or unsliced, in plastic wrap and place it in a freezer-safe bag. Freeze for up to 3 months.

APPLE PIE QUICK BREAD

2 cups (260 g) Sharon's Gluten-Free Flour Blend (page 179)

1 tsp xanthan gum

1 tsp baking powder

½ tsp baking soda

½ tsp fine sea salt

1 tsp ground cinnamon

¼ tsp ground nutmeg

⅛ tsp allspice

½ cup (97 g) granulated sugar

2 large eggs, room temperature

⅔ cup (160 ml) unsweetened coconut milk, room temperature

¼ cup (55 g) light brown sugar, packed

⅓ cup (80 ml) avocado oil

1 tsp pure vanilla extract

1 cup (250 g) prepared gluten-free, dairy-free apple pie filling

The layered effect of this bread slightly resembles an apple pie with the quick bread acting as the "crust." It's a fun seasonal take on a classic recipe. I use Lucky Leaf brand pie filling, which is gluten-free and dairy-free. If you use a homemade apple pie filling in place of the canned pie filling, it must be cooked and thickened. If the apples are raw, they will give off too much liquid during the baking process and the bread will not bake correctly.

Preheat the oven to 350°F (177°C) and spray a 9 x 5–inch (23 x 13–cm) loaf pan with nonstick spray or coat with homemade pan release (page 180). Then line with parchment paper and set aside.

In a large bowl, whisk together the gluten-free flour blend, xanthan gum, baking powder, baking soda, salt, cinnamon, nutmeg, allspice and granulated sugar. Set this aside.

In a medium bowl, whisk together the eggs, coconut milk, brown sugar, oil and vanilla extract.

Pour the wet ingredients into the dry ingredients. Mix these until just combined.

Transfer half of the batter to the prepared baking pan, then top with the apple pie filling. Add the remaining bread batter, gently spreading it evenly in the pan.

Bake for 55 to 65 minutes or until a cake tester or toothpick inserted in the middle comes out clean. Cool it in the pan for 30 minutes, then remove the bread from the pan and cool completely on a wire rack.

STORAGE NOTE: Store the bread wrapped tightly in plastic wrap at room temperature for up to 3 days. To freeze it, tightly wrap the whole loaf, sliced or unsliced, in plastic wrap and place it in a freezer-safe bag. Freeze for up to 3 months.

PUMPKIN PECAN STREUSEL BREAD

This Pumpkin Pecan Streusel Bread is like a delicious cross between pumpkin bread and coffee cake. If the two had a baby, this would be it! The pecans add a nice subtle crunch and nuttiness while the pumpkin and pumpkin pie spice (page 179) really make this bread taste like fall. The pumpkin pie spice is my homemade blend and is used in both the bread and the streusel. Feel free to use up to a teaspoon more in the bread and up to ½ teaspoon more in the streusel if you really want to amp up that warm spice flavor.

FOR THE STREUSEL

6 tbsp (51 g) Sharon's Gluten-Free Flour Blend (page 179)

⅛ tsp xanthan gum

2 tbsp (28 g) light brown sugar, packed

1 tbsp (8 g) finely chopped pecans

½ tsp Homemade Pumpkin Pie Spice (page 179)

2 tbsp (27 g) coconut oil, measured solid then melted

FOR THE BREAD

2 cups (260 g) Sharon's Gluten-Free Flour Blend (page 179)

½ tsp xanthan gum

1 tsp aluminum-free baking powder

½ tsp baking soda

½ tsp fine sea salt

2 tsp (3 g) Homemade Pumpkin Pie Spice (page 179)

½ cup (60 g) chopped pecans

2 large eggs, room temperature

1 cup (270 g) pumpkin puree

¾ cup (168 g) light brown sugar

½ cup (120 ml) unsweetened coconut milk

⅓ cup (80 ml) avocado oil

1 tsp pure vanilla extract

Preheat the oven to 350°F (177°C) and spray a 9 x 5–inch (23 x 13–cm) loaf pan with nonstick spray or coat with homemade pan release (page 180), then line it with a piece of parchment paper, leaving enough of an overhang to pull the bread out of the pan.

To make the streusel, stir together the gluten-free flour blend, xanthan gum, brown sugar, pecans and pumpkin pie spice in a small bowl. Stir in the melted coconut oil until the mixture is thick and slightly crumbly. Set this aside. This will dry and form a better crumb as it sits.

To make the bread, in a large bowl, whisk together the gluten-free flour blend, xanthan gum, baking powder, baking soda, salt and pumpkin pie spice. Next, stir in the chopped pecans and set aside.

In a medium bowl, whisk together the eggs, pumpkin puree, brown sugar, coconut milk, oil and vanilla extract.

Pour the wet ingredients into the dry ingredients and stir until combined.

Transfer the batter to the prepared loaf pan, spreading it evenly. Crumble the streusel over the top of the bread, distributing it evenly across the top.

Bake for 55 to 65 minutes or until a tester inserted in the middle comes out clean. Cool it in the pan for 20 minutes, then use the parchment paper to lift the bread out of the pan and cool on a wire rack (removing the parchment paper). Cool completely before slicing.

STORAGE NOTE: Store the bread wrapped tightly in plastic wrap at room temperature for up to 3 days. To freeze it, tightly wrap the whole loaf, sliced or unsliced, in plastic wrap and place it in a freezer-safe bag. Freeze for up to 3 months.

ICED GINGERBREAD LOAF

FOR THE BREAD

2 cups (260 g) Sharon's Gluten-Free Flour Blend (page 179)

1 tsp xanthan gum

1 tsp baking soda

½ tsp fine sea salt

1½ tsp (3 g) ground ginger

1 tsp ground cinnamon

¼ tsp ground nutmeg

¼ tsp ground cloves

2 large eggs, room temperature

½ cup (112 g) light brown sugar

¼ cup (60 ml) molasses (not blackstrap)

1 cup (240 ml) unsweetened coconut milk

⅓ cup (80 ml) avocado oil

1 tbsp (15 ml) white vinegar

½ tsp pure vanilla extract

FOR THE ICING

1 tbsp (15 g) vegan butter

1 tbsp (12 g) shortening

2 oz (57 g) dairy-free cream cheese

¾ cup (99 g) powdered sugar

¼ tsp pure vanilla extract

This bread literally smells like the holiday season. The warm spices that waft out of the oven as this loaf bakes are simply irresistible. I top this loaf with a creamy, smooth dairy-free cream cheese icing. It complements the spice in the bread so well! If you prefer to keep things a bit simpler, leave the loaf plain or give it a quick dusting of confectioners' sugar. Be sure to use regular, plain old molasses in this and not blackstrap molasses. I use Grandma's brand molasses here, but any brand will do as long as it is not blackstrap.

Preheat the oven to 350°F (177°C) and spray a 9 x 5–inch (23 x 13–cm) loaf pan with nonstick spray or coat with homemade pan release (page 180), then line it with parchment paper.

In a large bowl, whisk together the gluten-free flour blend, xanthan gum, baking soda, salt, ground ginger, cinnamon, nutmeg and cloves. Set this mixture aside.

In a medium bowl, whisk together the eggs, brown sugar, molasses, coconut milk, oil, vinegar and vanilla extract.

Pour the wet ingredients into the dry ingredients and stir them until combined. Transfer the batter to the prepared loaf pan, spreading it evenly. Bake it for 50 to 60 minutes or until a tester or toothpick inserted in the middle comes out clean.

Cool in the pan for 20 minutes, then remove from the pan and parchment paper and cool completely on a wire rack before frosting.

To make the icing, add the vegan butter, shortening, dairy-free cream cheese, powdered sugar and vanilla extract to a medium bowl. Use a hand mixer and beat on low speed to combine. Once the powdered sugar is incorporated, beat on medium speed until it's light and fluffy. Spread this on the cooled bread.

STORAGE NOTES: Keep covered in an airtight container at room temperature for up to 2 days. To freeze without the icing, wrap tightly in plastic wrap and then place in a freezer-safe bag. Freeze the loaf for up to 3 months. You can slice it before wrapping and freezing.

To freeze with the icing, slice and place bread flat on a sheet pan and freeze until solid. Wrap each slice in plastic wrap and then store in a freezer-safe bag. Defrost at room temperature.

CRANBERRY SWIRL BREAD

While Classic(ish) Cranberry Bread (page 139) is a must-make recipe during the holiday season, it's nice to change things up a bit! Wow your friends and family with this gorgeous twist.

FOR THE CRANBERRY COMPOTE

1½ cups (165 g) fresh or frozen cranberries

⅓ cup (65 g) granulated sugar

2 tsp (5 g) cornstarch

⅓ cup (80 ml) water

FOR THE BREAD

2 cups (260 g) Sharon's Gluten-Free Flour Blend (page 179)

1 tsp xanthan gum

1 tsp aluminum-free baking powder

½ tsp baking soda

½ tsp fine sea salt

½ cup (97 g) granulated sugar

2 large eggs, room temperature

¼ cup (55 g) light brown sugar, packed

⅔ cup (160 ml) unsweetened coconut milk, room temperature

⅓ cup (80 ml) avocado oil

1 tsp pure vanilla extract

1 tsp almond extract

FOR THE GLAZE

½ cup (66 g) powdered sugar

½ tsp almond extract

½ tsp pure vanilla extract

1 tsp unsweetened coconut milk

To make the compote, add the cranberries, granulated sugar, cornstarch and water to a medium saucepan and stir them together until the cornstarch is dissolved. Heat over medium-low heat until the cranberries have softened/popped and the liquid has thickened, about 10 minutes. Gently mash any whole cranberries. Set the compote aside and let it cool to room temperature.

Preheat the oven to 350°F (177°C) and spray a 9 x 5–inch (23 x 13–cm) loaf pan with nonstick spray or coat it with homemade pan release (page 180). Then line it with parchment paper and set aside.

In a large bowl, whisk together the gluten-free flour blend, xanthan gum, baking powder, baking soda, salt and granulated sugar. Set the mixture aside.

In a medium bowl, whisk together the eggs, brown sugar, coconut milk, oil, vanilla extract and almond extract. Pour the wet ingredients into the dry ingredients. Mix until they're just combined, then transfer half of the batter to the prepared baking pan.

Reserve ¼ cup (70 g) of the compote and then gently spread the remaining compote over the batter in the pan. Top with the remaining batter, spreading it evenly. Top with the reserved compote and swirl it into the bread.

Bake for 50 to 60 minutes or until a cake tester or toothpick inserted in the middle comes out clean. Cool it in the pan for 20 minutes, then remove the bread from the pan and parchment paper and cool completely on a wire rack.

To make the glaze, stir together the powdered sugar, almond extract, vanilla extract and coconut milk until smooth. Drizzle over the bread and let it set.

STORAGE NOTES: Keep the bread wrapped tightly in plastic wrap at room temperature for up to 3 days. To freeze, wrap tightly in plastic wrap, then freeze in a freezer-safe bag for up to 3 months.

To store the glazed bread, keep the bread covered in an airtight container. To freeze, slice the bread and freeze individual slices on a sheet pan. Then wrap individual slices in plastic wrap or transfer to sandwich bags before transferring to a freezer-safe bag. Remove bread from plastic wrap before defrosting on a plate at room temperature.

CHAMPAGNE BREAD

FOR THE BREAD

2 cups (260 g) Sharon's Gluten-Free Flour Blend (page 179)

1 tsp xanthan gum

2 tsp (7 g) aluminum-free baking powder

½ tsp fine sea salt

1 cup (195 g) granulated sugar

2 large eggs, room temperature

⅓ cup (80 ml) avocado oil

2 tsp (10 ml) pure vanilla extract

1 cup (240 ml) champagne, room temperature

FOR THE GLAZE

1 cup (132 g) powdered sugar

1 tbsp (15 ml) champagne

1 tsp pure vanilla extract

This is a really fun bread to make for holiday brunch. Using dry champagne is okay, but I find that a brut champagne works best in this recipe. It really enhances the sweetness of the bread, giving you a nice, subtly sweet champagne flavor. I like to use the smaller-sized bottles of champagne when I don't feel like opening a full-sized bottle for this bread. Four-packs are usually available at almost all package stores (or wherever you buy your liquor/spirits). For a fun twist, try this with a little orange extract and zest, then top with the orange glaze from my Orange Poppy Seed Bread (page 100).

Preheat the oven to 350°F (177°C) and spray a 9 x 5–inch (23 x 13–cm) loaf pan with nonstick spray or coat with homemade pan release (page 180). Then line it with parchment paper and set aside.

In a large bowl, whisk together the gluten-free flour blend, xanthan gum, baking powder, salt and granulated sugar. Set this aside.

In a medium bowl, whisk together the eggs, oil and vanilla extract. Pour the mixture into the dry ingredients. Mix them together until mostly combined, then gently stir in the champagne.

Transfer the batter to the prepared baking pan.

Bake for 50 to 55 minutes or until a cake tester or toothpick inserted in the middle comes out clean. Cool in the pan for 20 minutes, then remove the bread from the pan and parchment paper and cool it completely on a wire rack before adding the glaze.

To make the glaze, add the powdered sugar, champagne and vanilla extract to a bowl. Stir these together until smooth and pourable. If the glaze is too thick, add 1 teaspoon of champagne at a time until it's thin enough to drizzle/spread.

STORAGE NOTES: Keep the bread covered in an airtight container at room temperature for up to 3 days. To freeze the glazed bread, slice into individual pieces, then freeze flat on a sheet pan. Then transfer the frozen slices to a freezer-safe bag and place wax paper between the layers of bread. Remove from the bag and defrost at room temperature.

To freeze the bread without glaze, wrap tightly in plastic wrap, then freeze in a freezer-safe bag for up to 3 months.

STRAWBERRY RHUBARB COFFEE CAKE BREAD

FOR THE FILLING

1 cup (154 g) fresh strawberries, diced

1 cup (140 g) fresh rhubarb, diced

2 tsp (10 ml) fresh lemon juice

⅓ cup (65 g) granulated sugar

1 tbsp (8 g) cornstarch

FOR THE CRUMB TOPPING

6 tbsp (51 g) Sharon's Gluten-Free Flour Blend (page 179)

2 tbsp (24 g) granulated sugar

⅛ tsp xanthan gum

2 tbsp (27 g) coconut oil, measured solid then melted

FOR THE BREAD

2 cups (260 g) Sharon's Gluten-Free Flour Blend (page 179)

1 tsp xanthan gum

⅔ cup (130 g) granulated sugar

1½ tsp (5 g) baking powder

½ tsp baking soda

½ tsp fine sea salt

½ cup (90 g) palm shortening

2 large eggs, room temperature

1 cup (240 ml) unsweetened coconut milk, room temperature

2 tsp (10 ml) white vinegar

1 tsp pure vanilla extract

A seasonal favorite—strawberry rhubarb! While at first glance this quick bread looks long and complicated, it really is easy. When baking, the bread will rise high in the pan. Be sure to use a loaf pan with high sides. If you're concerned about some of the filling overflowing and dripping in your oven, place a cookie sheet on the rack below the bread.

To make the filling, add the strawberries, rhubarb and lemon juice to a medium-sized saucepan; cover and cook over medium heat for 5 minutes. Stir in the sugar and cornstarch and bring to a boil. Cook until the strawberries are soft and mashable, about 3 to 5 minutes. Remove the pan from the heat and let it cool.

To make the crumb topping, stir together the gluten-free flour, granulated sugar and xanthan gum. Stir in the melted coconut oil until it's well incorporated. Set this aside.

To make the bread, preheat the oven to 350°F (177°C) and spray a 9 x 5 x 3–inch (23 x 13 x 7.5–cm) loaf pan with nonstick spray or coat with homemade pan release (page 180), then line it with parchment paper, leaving enough of an overhang to pull the bread out of the pan.

In a large bowl, whisk together the gluten-free flour, xanthan gum, granulated sugar, baking powder, baking soda and salt. Add the palm shortening and use a fork to cut it into the flour mixture until it resembles fine crumbs. Set it aside.

In a medium bowl, whisk together the eggs, coconut milk, vinegar and vanilla extract. Pour the wet ingredients into the dry ingredients and stir until just combined.

Pour half of the batter into the prepared pan. Top with the cooled filling, spreading it evenly over the batter. Top with the remaining batter, carefully spreading it evenly. Top the batter with the crumb topping. Bake for 50 to 60 minutes or until a cake tester inserted in the middle comes out clean. Cool in the pan for 30 minutes, then use the parchment paper to lift the bread out of the pan and cool on a wire rack for at least an hour before slicing.

STORAGE NOTE: To store, keep tightly wrapped in plastic wrap at room temperature for up to 3 days. To freeze, wrap tightly in plastic wrap and then place in a freezer-safe bag. Freeze the loaf for up to 3 months. You can slice it before wrapping and freezing.

ZUCCHINI BREAD

2 cups (260 g) Sharon's Gluten-Free Flour Blend (page 179)

1 tsp xanthan gum

1 tsp aluminum-free baking powder

½ tsp baking soda

½ tsp fine sea salt

1½ tsp (4 g) ground cinnamon

2 large eggs, room temperature

⅔ cup (130 g) light brown sugar, packed

½ cup (120 ml) unsweetened coconut milk, room temperature

⅓ cup (80 ml) avocado oil

1 tsp pure vanilla extract

2 cups (200 g) grated zucchini

I had been planning to have a gluten-free zucchini bread recipe on my blog for a couple of years now, but each year came and went and I just wasn't able to get to it. Zucchini bread is such a classic recipe, right up there with Truly, the Best Ever Gluten-Free Banana Nut Bread (page 12). Everyone has their own favorite family recipe for zucchini bread, and this is my version made gluten- and dairy-free. If you like baking with zucchini, be sure to try the Chocolate Zucchini Bread (page 52), Lemon Zucchini Bread (page 104) and Zucchini Banana Bread (page 28). Just a heads-up—there's no need to take the extra step of squeezing out any extra liquid from the zucchini. This recipe relies on that moisture.

Preheat the oven to 350°F (177°C) and spray a 9 x 5–inch (23 x 13–cm) loaf pan with nonstick spray or coat with homemade pan release (page 180), then line it with parchment paper.

In a large bowl, whisk together the gluten-free flour blend, xanthan gum, baking powder, baking soda, salt and cinnamon. Set the mixture aside.

In a medium bowl, whisk together the eggs, brown sugar, coconut milk, oil and vanilla extract.

Pour the wet ingredients into the dry ingredients. Mix them until just combined, then fold in the grated zucchini.

Transfer the batter to the prepared baking pan.

Bake for 50 to 60 minutes or until a cake tester or toothpick inserted in the middle comes out clean. Cool it in the pan for 20 minutes, then cool completely on a wire rack.

STORAGE NOTE: Store the bread, wrapped tightly in plastic wrap, at room temperature for up to 3 days. To freeze it, tightly wrap the whole loaf, sliced or unsliced, in plastic wrap and place it in a freezer-safe bag. Freeze it for up to 3 months.

SWEET PEACH BREAD

FOR THE PEACH COMPOTE

1½ cups (210 g) peaches, thinly sliced

¼ cup (55 g) light brown sugar, packed

1 tsp fresh lemon juice

½ tsp ground cinnamon

FOR THE BREAD

2 cups (260 g) Sharon's Gluten-Free Flour Blend (page 179)

¾ tsp xanthan gum

1 tsp aluminum-free baking powder

½ tsp baking soda

½ tsp fine sea salt

¾ cup (146 g) granulated sugar

2 large eggs, room temperature

⅔ cup (160 ml) unsweetened coconut milk, room temperature

½ cup (123 g) dairy-free plain or vanilla yogurt

⅓ cup (80 ml) avocado oil

1½ tsp (7 ml) pure vanilla extract

The flavor of this bread reminds me of peach kuchen, a dessert my mom used to make when we were kids. It had a shortbread-like crust made out of cake mix and margarine, and it was topped with sliced peaches, a sweet sour cream mixture and cinnamon. It was outstanding. The yogurt, combined with the peaches and cinnamon in this recipe, brings in all of the flavors from that tasty dessert. You can use fresh, in-season peaches or canned peaches here. I prefer fresh. If using canned, be sure to drain the peaches well and rinse off any of the syrup.

To make the peach compote, add the peaches, brown sugar, lemon juice and cinnamon to a nonstick skillet. Heat over medium heat for 5 minutes until the peaches are soft and the sugar is thick and syrupy. Set this aside and cool to room temperature.

Preheat the oven to 350°F (177°C) and spray a 9 x 5–inch (23 x 13–cm) loaf pan with nonstick spray or coat with homemade pan release (page 180). Then line it with parchment paper and set aside.

In a large bowl, whisk together the gluten-free flour blend, xanthan gum, baking powder, baking soda, salt and granulated sugar. Set the mixture aside.

In a medium bowl, whisk together the eggs, coconut milk, yogurt, oil and vanilla extract.

Pour the wet ingredients into the dry ingredients and mix them until just combined. Fold in the cooled peach compote.

Transfer the batter to the prepared baking pan.

Bake for 50 to 65 minutes or until a cake tester or toothpick inserted in the middle comes out clean. Cool it in the pan for 20 minutes, then remove the bread from the pan and parchment paper and cool completely on a wire rack.

STORAGE NOTE: Store the bread wrapped tightly in plastic wrap at room temperature for up to 3 days. To freeze it, tightly wrap the whole loaf, sliced or unsliced, in plastic wrap and place it in a freezer-safe bag. Freeze for up to 3 months.

FUSS-FREE SPECIALTY BREADS

LOAVES WITH A TWIST

The breads in this chapter are fun and flavor-packed! Each one brings something special to your kitchen, whether it's a schmear of marshmallow fluff or a dash of matcha. They're perfect for when you feel like changing things up or experimenting a bit. This is also the only chapter in the book that includes quick breads that aren't baked in a traditional loaf pan. Both the Green Chile Cornbread (page 170) and Honey Cornbread (page 162) are baked in a square baking pan, while the Gluten-Free Frybread (page 173) is fried in a skillet on the stove-top. These breads make great additions to the dinner table because they can be made quickly and served hot, warm or room temperature.

PANCAKE BREAD

2 cups (260 g) Sharon's Gluten-Free Flour Blend (page 179)

½ tsp xanthan gum

2 tsp (7 g) aluminum-free baking powder

½ tsp fine sea salt

½ cup (97 g) granulated sugar

2 large eggs, room temperature

1 cup (240 ml) unsweetened coconut milk, room temperature

¼ cup (60 ml) avocado oil

2 tbsp (30 ml) pure maple syrup

1 tsp pure vanilla extract

1 tsp butter extract

If you've ever wished you had time for pancakes on a busy weekday morning, this is your solution! This bread tastes just like pancakes but is portable and doesn't require a fork and plate. Make this ahead of time and freeze individual slices for easy portioning, then defrost what you need as you need it. You can serve this two ways: sliced and plain or toasted with your dairy-free butter of choice, fresh berries and a drizzle of pure maple syrup. If you're looking for a stronger maple flavor, replace the pure maple syrup with 1 tablespoon (15 ml) of coconut milk plus 1 teaspoon of maple extract.

Preheat the oven to 350°F (177°C) and spray a 9 x 5–inch (23 x 13–cm) loaf pan with nonstick spray or coat with homemade pan release (page 180). Then line it with parchment paper and set aside.

In a large bowl, whisk together the gluten-free flour blend, xanthan gum, baking powder, salt and granulated sugar. Set this aside.

In a medium bowl, whisk together the eggs, coconut milk, oil, maple syrup, vanilla extract and butter extract.

Pour the wet ingredients into the dry ingredients. Mix them until just combined, then transfer the batter to the prepared baking pan.

Bake for 50 to 60 minutes or until a cake tester or toothpick inserted in the middle comes out clean. Cool it in the pan for 20 minutes, then remove the bread from the pan and parchment paper and cool completely on a wire rack.

STORAGE NOTE: Store the bread wrapped tightly in plastic wrap at room temperature for up to 3 days. To freeze it, tightly wrap the whole loaf, sliced or unsliced, in plastic wrap and place it in a freezer-safe bag. Freeze for up to 3 months.

FLUFFERNUTTER BREAD

2 cups (260 g) Sharon's Gluten-Free Flour Blend (page 179)

1 tsp xanthan gum

1 tsp aluminum-free baking powder

½ tsp baking soda

½ tsp fine sea salt

½ cup (97 g) granulated sugar

2 large eggs, room temperature

½ cup (112 g) light brown sugar, packed

1 cup (240 ml) unsweetened coconut milk, room temperature

¼ cup (60 ml) avocado oil

1 tsp pure vanilla extra

½ cup (91 g) creamy peanut butter

½ cup (65 g) marshmallow fluff or marshmallow crème

Fluffernutters have long been a staple in children's lunchboxes throughout New England. If you've never heard of a fluffernutter, it's a peanut butter and marshmallow fluff sandwich. It's sticky, salty and sweet. Marshmallow fluff is a product that's prevalent in New England, but you can also buy marshmallow crème which is usually found in the same aisle at the grocery store as the peanut butter and jelly. When baked, the fluff will dissolve into the bread batter but the flavor will still be there. It tastes just like the sandwiches I used to enjoy as a kid.

Preheat the oven to 350°F (177°C) and spray a 9 x 5–inch (23 x 13–cm) loaf pan with nonstick spray or coat with homemade pan release (page 180). Then line it with parchment paper and set aside.

In a large bowl, whisk together the gluten-free flour blend, xanthan gum, baking powder, baking soda, salt and granulated sugar. Set the mixture aside.

In a medium bowl, whisk together the eggs, brown sugar, coconut milk, oil and vanilla extract. Set this aside.

Melt the peanut butter in a microwave-safe bowl, heating for 20 seconds until it's thin enough to pour. Whisk the peanut butter into the wet ingredients and then whisk in the fluff until it's mostly combined. Small chunks of marshmallow fluff in the liquid are fine.

Pour the wet ingredients into the dry ingredients. Mix them until just combined, then transfer the batter to the prepared baking pan.

Bake for 50 to 60 minutes or until a cake tester or toothpick inserted in the middle comes out clean. Cool it in the pan for 20 minutes, then remove the bread from the pan and parchment paper and cool completely on a wire rack.

STORAGE NOTE Store the bread wrapped tightly in plastic wrap at room temperature for up to 3 days. To freeze it, tightly wrap the whole loaf, sliced or unsliced, in plastic wrap and place it in a freezer-safe bag. Freeze for up to 3 months.

HONEY CORNBREAD

1¼ cups (163 g) Sharon's Gluten-Free Flour Blend (page 179)

½ tsp xanthan gum

¾ cup (130 g) cornmeal (use finely ground for best results)

2 tsp (7 g) aluminum-free baking powder

½ tsp fine sea salt

1 large egg, room temperature

1 cup (240 ml) unsweetened coconut milk, room temperature

¼ cup (60 ml) avocado oil

¼ cup (60 ml) honey

Cornbread is a hot commodity in my house. My kids and husband absolutely love it, so when I make it, it hardly lasts. I find that the best cornbread is made with finely ground cornmeal. If you have a coarse ground cornmeal, just run it through a food processor to reach the desired consistency. Some honey comes in a more solid state, so be sure to use honey that's in liquid form. You want to be able to whisk it into the dry ingredients, and solid honey won't be easy to mix in.

Preheat the oven to 400°F (204°C) and spray an 8 x 8–inch (20 x 20–cm) pan with nonstick spray or coat with homemade pan release (page 180).

In a large bowl, whisk together the gluten-free flour blend, xanthan gum, cornmeal, baking powder and salt. Set this aside.

In a separate small bowl, whisk together the egg, coconut milk, oil and honey. Pour the wet ingredients into the dry ingredients and mix them until incorporated. Pour the batter into the prepared pan, spreading it evenly.

Bake for 20 to 24 minutes. You can serve this bread hot or at room temperature.

STORAGE NOTE: Keep tightly covered at room temperature up to 2 days. Individual slices can also be frozen.

CHAI TEA BREAD

2 cups (260 g) Sharon's Gluten-Free Flour Blend (page 179)

1 tsp xanthan gum

1 tsp aluminum-free baking powder

½ tsp baking soda

½ tsp fine sea salt

1½ tsp (3 g) Homemade Chai Spice Mix (page 180)

¼ cup (49 g) granulated sugar

2 large eggs, room temperature

½ cup (112 g) light brown sugar, packed

1 cup (240 ml) brewed chai tea, room temperature

⅓ cup (80 ml) avocado oil

2 tsp (10 ml) pure vanilla extract

I made this bread with my mom in mind because we always have chai tea in the house for her. I'm not much of a tea drinker—I'm a coffee girl through-and-through—but I really love this bread. The mild chai spice blend, along with the extra flavor from the chai tea baked right into the bread, makes you feel like cozying up with a good book by the fire . . . or with an iced chai latte on the back deck of the pool since this bread is good any time of the year!

Preheat the oven to 350°F (177°C) and spray a 9 x 5–inch (23 x 13–cm) loaf pan with nonstick spray or coat with homemade pan release (page 180). Then line it with parchment paper and set aside.

In a large bowl, whisk together the gluten-free flour blend, xanthan gum, baking powder, baking soda, salt, chai spice mix and granulated sugar. Set the mixture aside.

In a medium bowl, whisk together the eggs, brown sugar, chai tea, oil and vanilla extract.

Pour the wet ingredients into the dry ingredients. Mix until they are just combined, then transfer the batter to the prepared baking pan.

Bake for 50 to 60 minutes or until a cake tester or toothpick inserted in the middle comes out clean. Cool it in the pan for 20 minutes, then remove the bread from the pan and parchment paper and cool completely on a wire rack.

STORAGE NOTES Store the bread wrapped tightly in plastic wrap at room temperature for up to 3 days. To freeze it, tightly wrap the whole loaf, sliced or unsliced, in plastic wrap and place it in a freezer-safe bag. Freeze for up to 3 months.

COFFEE CAKE QUICK BREAD

Coffee Cake Quick Bread is easier and faster than making a larger coffee cake, so it's a great way to satisfy that coffee cake craving without having to make an entire pan or cake large enough to feed a big crowd. This quick bread version has a slightly denser base than the cake version, making it a great choice for portability. It's also got a generous crumb-to-bread ratio since there's crumb in the bread and on top. It's the best part anyway, so the double crumb is the way to go!

FOR THE CRUMB TOPPING

¾ cup (100 g) Sharon's Gluten-Free Flour Blend (page 179)

¼ cup (55 g) light brown sugar, packed

¼ tsp xanthan gum

1 tsp ground cinnamon

¼ cup (55 g) refined coconut oil, measured solid then melted

FOR THE BREAD

2 cups (260 g) Sharon's Gluten-Free Flour Blend (page 179)

1 tsp xanthan gum

1 tsp aluminum-free baking powder

½ tsp baking soda

½ tsp fine sea salt

⅔ cup (130 g) granulated sugar

½ cup (90 g) shortening

2 large eggs, room temperature

⅔ cup (160 ml) unsweetened coconut milk, room temperature

1½ tsp (7 ml) pure vanilla extract

1 tsp butter extract

Preheat the oven to 350°F (177°C) and spray a 9 x 5–inch (23 x 13–cm) loaf pan with nonstick spray or coat with homemade pan release (page 180). Then line it with parchment paper and set aside.

To make the crumb topping, stir together the gluten-free flour blend, light brown sugar, xanthan gum and cinnamon. Stir in the melted coconut oil until crumbs have formed. Set this mixture aside.

To make the bread, whisk together the gluten-free flour blend, xanthan gum, baking powder, baking soda, salt and granulated sugar in a large bowl.

Add the shortening, and cut it in with a fork until fine crumbs have formed, then set it aside.

In a medium bowl, whisk together the eggs, coconut milk, vanilla extract and butter extract.

Pour the wet ingredients into the dry ingredients and mix until they are just combined.

Transfer half of the batter to the prepared baking pan, then top with half of the crumb topping. Add the remaining bread batter and spread it evenly in the pan. Top with the remaining crumb topping.

Bake for 50 to 60 minutes or until a cake tester or toothpick inserted in the middle comes out clean. Cool it in the pan for 20 minutes, then remove the bread from the pan and parchment paper and cool completely on a wire rack.

STORAGE NOTE: Store the bread wrapped tightly in plastic wrap at room temperature for up to 3 days. To freeze it, tightly wrap the whole loaf, sliced or unsliced, in plastic wrap and place it in a freezer-safe bag. Freeze for up to 3 months.

MATCHA QUICK BREAD

2 cups (260 g) Sharon's Gluten-Free Flour Blend (page 179)

1 tsp xanthan gum

1 tsp aluminum-free baking powder

½ tsp baking soda

½ tsp fine sea salt

1 cup (195 g) granulated sugar

1–2 tbsp (5–10 g) matcha powder

2 large eggs, room temperature

1 cup (240 ml) unsweetened coconut milk, room temperature

⅓ cup (80 ml) avocado oil

1½ tsp (7 ml) pure vanilla extract

There's a food craze that has taken over the internet and social media—matcha everything. While matcha (pronounced "MAH-cha") has been used for centuries in Japanese tea ceremonies, you will now see it in the form of baked goods, ice creams, drinks (aside from the traditional tea service), candy and so much more. This is my take on using it as a "trendy" ingredient in a different way. The matcha tea provides a really unique flavor to the bread and also gives it a fun green hue. For a stronger green tea flavor and deeper green bread, use an additional 1 tablespoon (5 g) of matcha powder. I recommend using culinary-grade matcha powder. It's great for baking and is usually less expensive than what's used for ceremonial tea.

Preheat the oven to 350°F (177°C) and spray a 9 x 5–inch (23 x 13–cm) loaf pan with nonstick spray or coat with homemade pan release (page 180). Then line it with parchment paper and set aside.

In a large bowl, whisk together the gluten-free flour blend, xanthan gum, baking powder, baking soda, salt, sugar and matcha powder. Set the mixture aside.

In a medium bowl, whisk together the eggs, coconut milk, oil and vanilla extract.

Pour the wet ingredients into the dry ingredients. Mix them until just combined, then transfer the batter to the prepared baking pan.

Bake for 50 to 60 minutes or until a cake tester or toothpick inserted in the middle comes out clean. Cool it in the pan for 20 minutes, then remove the bread from the pan and parchment paper and cool completely on a wire rack.

STORAGE NOTE: Store the bread wrapped tightly in plastic wrap at room temperature for up to 3 days. To freeze it, tightly wrap the whole loaf, sliced or unsliced, in plastic wrap and place it in a freezer-safe bag. Freeze for up to 3 months.

GREEN CHILE CORNBREAD

1¼ cups (163 g) Sharon's Gluten-Free Flour Blend (page 179)

¾ tsp xanthan gum

¾ cup (130 g) cornmeal (use finely ground for best results)

¼ cup (49 g) granulated sugar

2 tsp (7 g) aluminum-free baking powder

½ tsp fine sea salt

1 large egg, room temperature

1 cup (240 ml) unsweetened coconut milk, room temperature

¼ cup (60 ml) avocado oil

4 oz (113 g) canned green chile peppers

This is a variation of the popular cornbread recipe on my blog. While that one is a classic, this one has a fun, spicy twist—green chile peppers. I get the canned fire-roasted peppers, which can easily be found at any grocery store. Since this is a savory bread, it would go great as a side dish for a chili or barbecue. I like to top mine with a bit of dairy-free butter and a drizzle of local honey. That sweet and spicy combo is fantastic. I highly recommend it!

Preheat the oven to 400°F (204°C) and spray an 8 x 8–inch (20 x 20–cm) pan with nonstick spray or coat with homemade pan release (page 180).

In a large bowl, whisk together the gluten-free flour blend, xanthan gum, cornmeal, sugar, baking powder and salt. Set this mixture aside.

In a separate small bowl, whisk together the egg, coconut milk, oil and chile peppers. Pour the wet ingredients into the dry ingredients and mix them until they're incorporated. Pour the batter into the prepared pan, spreading it evenly.

Bake for 20 to 24 minutes. You can serve this bread hot or at room temperature.

STORAGE NOTE: Keep tightly covered at room temperature up to 2 days. Individual slices can also be frozen.

GLUTEN-FREE FRYBREAD

1½ cups (195 g) Sharon's Gluten-Free Flour Blend (page 179)

½ cup (64 g) cassava flour

1 tsp xanthan gum

2 tsp (7 g) aluminum-free baking powder

½ tsp fine sea salt

1 cup (240 ml) warm water

Shortening or oil, for frying

If you haven't heard of frybread, it is a flat bread made with simple ingredients and fried in a skillet. The origins of this recipe have deep roots dating back to "The Long Walk." I encourage you to research and read the history of this recipe and how it came to be. Frybread is usually served with taco meat or chili and/or beans, but you can also make a sweet version and top it with cinnamon and sugar as soon as it's cooked. The heat will melt the sugar and cinnamon into the bread—that's my favorite way to eat it. It's very similar to the fried dough that you'd get at a fair. I use cassava flour in this recipe to add chewiness to the bread.

In a large bowl, whisk together the gluten-free flour blend, cassava flour, xanthan gum, baking powder and salt.

Stir in the water and mix until just combined. Use your hand to knead the dough together until it forms a ball.

Divide the dough into 6 balls. Cover the dough balls with plastic wrap so they don't dry out.

Heat 1 inch (2.5 cm) of oil or shortening in a deep-sided cast-iron pan and heat it to 350 to 375°F (177 to 191°C).

Roll 1 ball of dough out between two pieces of plastic wrap until it's about 5 to 6 inches (13 to 15 cm) in diameter. When the oil is hot, remove the dough from the plastic wrap and carefully lower it into the hot oil. Fry it until golden brown, then flip and fry the other side.

Repeat with the remaining dough balls, keeping them covered in plastic until ready to fry.

Drain the frybread on paper towels, then serve immediately with toppings of choice.

QUICK BREAD TRANSFORMATION

Have you ever baked something and wondered how you can take it to the next level? In this chapter, you will find three simple and totally delicious ways to elevate your gluten-free, dairy-free quick breads by turning them into something new and unique. Instead of using store-bought sandwich bread for French toast, try it with quick bread! I've shared my family's favorite easy French Toast recipe (page 176) along with a stuffed French toast bake (page 177), bread pudding (page 175) and the best quick breads to try with each recipe.

BREAD PUDDING MADE WITH QUICK BREAD

1 loaf quick bread, baked, cooled and cut into cubes

2 cups (480 ml) unsweetened coconut milk (see note)

4 large eggs, room temperature

½ cup (112 g) light brown sugar, packed

1½ tsp (7 ml) pure vanilla extract

Bread pudding is a great dessert option if you're looking to make something different. I like it with a little bit of homemade whipped cream (regular or coconut) or vanilla ice cream (regular or dairy-free). This includes a basic custard recipe, but feel free to experiment with different flavors, spices, ½ cup of mix-ins (like chocolate or fruit) or different extracts depending on which quick bread you use. This recipe is also great for using up leftover quick breads as drier bread works best here. If you're using freshly made bread, just toast it in the oven on a sheet pan once it's cubed to dry it out a bit. If the bread is too moist, it won't soak up the custard as well.

Preheat the oven to 350°F (177°C) and spray an 8 x 8–inch (20 x 20–cm) baking dish with nonstick spray or coat with homemade pan release (page 180). Then line it with parchment paper and set aside.

Add the cubed bread to the prepared baking pan, spreading it evenly throughout.

In a medium bowl, whisk together the coconut milk, eggs, sugar and vanilla until it's well combined. Pour this mixture over the bread.

Use a fork or spoon to gently press the bread into the pan to submerge it in the liquid. Let it sit for 10 minutes before baking.

Bake for 40 to 45 minutes or until the middle is just set. Serve the bread warm with desired toppings.

NOTE: For a richer custard, use full-fat coconut milk.

FRENCH TOAST MADE WITH QUICK BREAD

4 large eggs

1½ tsp (7 ml) pure vanilla extract

1 tsp almond extract

½ tsp ground cinnamon

¼ tsp ground nutmeg

1 cup (240 ml) unsweetened coconut milk

1 loaf quick bread of choice, baked and cooled

Pure maple syrup, for serving

Chopped nuts, for serving, optional

Fresh fruit, for serving, optional

I like to make French toast with quick breads for special brunches. Since quick bread is more delicate than doughy yeast bread, the slices need to be thicker and you need to be gentle when dipping and flipping. Some breads hold up better than others, and breads with lots of swirls or mix-ins are more likely to fall apart. Stick to firmer breads like banana breads, chocolate breads, cake-like breads or pumpkin/sweet potato breads.

In a medium bowl, whisk together the eggs, vanilla extract, almond extract, cinnamon and nutmeg. Once the cinnamon is incorporated into the eggs, whisk in the coconut milk, then set the mixture aside.

Slice the quick bread into 10 slices and set it aside. Preheat griddle to medium-low heat and grease it if necessary.

Submerge a piece of bread in the custard, coating all sides.

Place the bread on your hot griddle and cook until each side is nicely browned and hot, about 3 minutes per side. Repeat for each piece of bread, cooking in batches if necessary.

Serve hot with pure maple syrup and garnish with chopped nuts and fresh fruit of choice if desired.

STUFFED FRENCH TOAST BAKE

This spectacular twist on French toast casserole is perfect for holidays and Sunday brunch. It's sweet, creamy and a total breakfast comfort food. Top it with pure maple syrup and OMG I'm sold. Since the custard in this recipe includes cinnamon and nutmeg, the best quick breads to use here are the ones that either already contain those spices or would pair well with them. If you want to use any of the chocolate breads for this, I suggest omitting the spices and using more vanilla extract in place of the almond extract. Some of my favorite breads to use with this recipe are the pumpkin breads, Cinnamon Swirl Bread (page 63), Sweet Potato Bread (page 136), banana breads and fruit-filled breads.

FOR THE CUSTARD

4 large eggs

1½ tsp (7 ml) pure vanilla extract

1 tsp almond extract

½ tsp ground cinnamon

¼ tsp ground nutmeg

1 cup (240 ml) unsweetened coconut milk

FOR THE FILLING

8 oz (227 g) dairy-free cream cheese

2 large eggs, room temperature

⅔ cup (130 g) granulated sugar

½ cup (65 g) Sharon's Gluten-Free Flour Blend (page 179)

1 tsp pure vanilla extract

FOR THE FRENCH TOAST

1 loaf quick bread, baked and cooled

2 tbsp (28 g) turbinado sugar

Pure maple syrup, for serving

Fresh fruit, for serving, optional

Preheat the oven to 350°F (177°C) and coat a 9 x 5–inch (23 x 13–cm) loaf pan with homemade pan release (page 180) or spray with nonstick spray.

To make the custard, add the eggs, vanilla extract, almond extract, cinnamon and nutmeg to a medium bowl and whisk together. Once the cinnamon is incorporated into the eggs, whisk in the coconut milk then set the mixture aside.

To make the filling, add the dairy-free cream cheese and eggs to a medium bowl. Use a hand mixer to beat until smooth and creamy, about 1 to 2 minutes. Add the granulated sugar, gluten-free flour blend and vanilla extract. Beat this another minute until smooth. Set it aside.

Slice the quick bread into 10 to 12 pieces, no thicker than sandwich bread—you will not use the whole loaf.

Place an even layer of bread in the bottom of the pan, cutting the bread as necessary to fit. Top with half of the cream cheese mixture.

Add another layer of bread, cutting it to fit, and cover the cream cheese layer. Add the remaining cream cheese, spreading it evenly over the bread. Add the top layer of bread, covering the cream cheese completely.

Whisk the custard, then carefully and slowly pour over the bread.

Sprinkle the top with the turbinado sugar. Bake for 45 minutes or until set. The custard might bubble up the sides a bit and that's fine!

Slice into 12 pieces or 8 squares and serve with pure maple syrup and fresh fruit if desired.

I'M BRINGING BAKING BACK

(TO GLUTEN-FREE KITCHENS)

This chapter includes some staple pantry recipes that are essential to some of the breads in this cookbook. The Gluten-Free Flour Blend (page 179) is my tried-and-true blend I used to develop every single one of these recipes. Once you try it, you'll wonder how you ever baked gluten-free without it. There are also some easy homemade spice blends made with spices you probably already have on hand that bring the breads in this book to the next level. I've even included a recipe for homemade pan release (page 180) since many store-bought nonstick sprays contain flour. These recipes are must-haves to make your gluten- and dairy-free baking dreams come true.

SHARON'S GLUTEN-FREE FLOUR BLEND

YIELD: 3 CUPS (410 G)

1 cup (165 g) white rice flour

1 cup (115 g) brown rice flour

⅔ cup (85 g) arrowroot powder

⅓ cup (45 g) tapioca flour/starch

This has been my go-to flour mix for the last couple of years, ever since I decided to experiment with arrowroot powder in place of the typical potato starch found in many gluten-free flour blends. I prefer using arrowroot because it yields a really great, soft texture in gluten-free baked goods that's very similar to their gluten-filled counterparts. I've found that arrowroot also binds better than potato starch, so I'm able to use a little less xanthan gum than what is typically recommended. This recipe makes 3 cups (410 g) of flour. I almost always double or triple this so I don't have to make it as often. Be sure to always stir your flour before measuring.

Add the white rice flour, brown rice flour, arrowroot powder and tapioca flour to an airtight container. Stir well, and if possible, shake the container to combine. Stir again and keep tightly covered until ready to use. I store my flour blend in a large container that has a lid.

If measuring with standard American measuring cups, use the "spoon and sweep" method (How to Measure Flour, page 182).

HOMEMADE PUMPKIN PIE SPICE

YIELD: 3½ TEASPOONS (6 G)

2 tsp (5 g) ground cinnamon

½ tsp ground nutmeg

½ tsp ground ginger

¼ tsp ground cloves

¼ tsp allspice

This recipe makes a small batch—3½ teaspoons (6 g)—of pumpkin pie spice, but feel free to double or even quadruple the recipe if you plan on using it frequently. I use it in the Chocolate Pumpkin Bread (page 55) and Pumpkin Pecan Streusel Bread (page 143), and I also like to make homemade pumpkin spice lattes with it. It's so fragrant and adds a great fall-inspired flavor to your drinks and baked goods.

Add the cinnamon, nutmeg, ginger, cloves and allspice to a small resealable container, such as a small mason jar. Mix it well. Store tightly covered at room temperature.

HOMEMADE PAN RELEASE

YIELD: 1¼ CUPS (300 ML)

½ cup (65 g) Sharon's Gluten-Free Flour Blend (page 179)

½ cup (90 g) shortening

½ cup (120 ml) avocado or canola oil

This is a great alternative to store-bought nonstick spray. I was a fan of the baking spray before I started baking gluten-free, but I can no longer use it since it contains flour. This recipe coats your pans with both fat- and gluten-free flour. It's great for all baked goods, especially Bundt cakes. This is a versatile recipe that can be halved or doubled according to your needs, but be sure to use equal portions of each ingredient. For chocolate-based recipes, you can use a chocolate-based pan release. Just substitute unsweetened cocoa powder for the gluten-free flour blend.

Add all ingredients to a medium bowl and whisk them together until completely combined.

Store in an airtight container, such as a mason jar.

Stir well before using and apply a generous amount to your baking pan with a pastry brush.

STORAGE NOTE: This can be stored at room temperature for a couple of weeks. Keep refrigerated for longer storage and if you're living in a hot or humid climate. If refrigerated, bring to room temperature before using.

HOMEMADE CHAI SPICE MIX

YIELD: ABOUT 2½ TABLESPOONS (18 G)

3 tsp (5 g) ground ginger

2 tsp (5 g) ground cinnamon

1 tsp ground cardamom

1 tsp ground allspice

1 tsp ground cloves

¼ tsp white pepper, optional

This is one of the main ingredients in my Chai Tea Bread (page 165). Most of the spices here are probably ones you already have in your pantry or spice cabinet. This blend can be used in muffins or some of the other quick breads in this book to give them a different flavor profile. It works well with the Banana Nut Bread (page 12), Pumpkin Pecan Streusel Bread (page 143), Sweet Potato Bread (page 136) or even Zucchini Bread (page 152).

Stir all ingredients until well combined. Store in an airtight container, such as a glass spice jar or small mason jar.

QUICK BREADS 101

Quick breads are some of the most popular baked goods around. They can be made quickly, and they're perfect for sharing with friends and family. To make the most out of your gluten-free and dairy-free loaves, I'm sharing some helpful tips on how to bake the perfect loaf, troubleshoot a dry bread and even how to easily turn your quick bread batter into muffins or mini breads. I also give you the rundown on all you need to know about some of the ingredients and brands I use to make these recipes. The How to Measure Flour (page 182) section may be small, but it's one of the most important sections to read since gluten-free flour is the base of every recipe in this book.

GLUTEN-FREE FLOUR

My special flour blend (page 179) consists of four types of gluten-free flours: brown rice flour, white rice flour, tapioca flour (or starch) and arrowroot powder. The arrowroot is used in place of potato starch, so this is a great flour blend for those who are sensitive to nightshades or those who have a potato allergy.

Bob's Red Mill 1:1 Gluten-Free Baking Flour can also be used in place of my flour blend. If you go this route, be sure to omit the xanthan gum called for in the recipe. Too much xanthan gum will cause the breads to have a very chewy, almost rubbery texture.

A NOTE ABOUT NIGHTSHADES

There is some misinformation out there about whether or not arrowroot and tapioca are nightshades. Tapioca comes from cassava root (sometimes called yuca root), which is not part of the nightshade family. Arrowroot is from the *Maranta arundinacea* (also known as the Marantaceae) family of plants, which are not part of the nightshade (Solanaceae) plant family.

XANTHAN GUM

Xanthan gum is a common ingredient in gluten-free baking and can be found in the same aisle as the gluten-free flours. It acts as a binder and gives the quick breads (and other gluten-free baked goods) the desired texture and structure of regular, gluten-filled breads. Too much xanthan gum isn't a good thing, so be sure to follow the recommended amount in each recipe and don't use more.

NONDAIRY MILK

Using coconut milk in place of regular dairy milk is one of the easiest swaps you can do to make baked goods dairy-free. I prefer using it over almond milk because it doesn't impart any flavor on the end product while nut milks will often give baked goods a slightly nutty flavor. I like to use unsweetened coconut milk, the kind found in the refrigerated section with the regular dairy milk. Shelf-stable cartons can also be used—just make sure you refrigerate them once they're opened!

A couple of the recipes in this cookbook call for full-fat coconut milk. That's the canned coconut milk that can be found in any grocery store. When you open the can, stir the milk really well to combine the coconut cream and coconut water because they separate in the can.

I also use walnut milk in some of the banana bread recipes and nut-based recipes. Walnut milk usually comes sweetened, so you can cut back on the sugar a bit in those recipes if you prefer (I usually don't).

If you have a nut or coconut allergy, use an unflavored and unsweetened rice milk.

AVOCADO OIL

A year or so ago, I switched from baking with canola or vegetable oil to baking with avocado oil, and I haven't looked back. It's a great high-temperature oil, so I use it for cooking and grilling, too. It's a solid staple to have in your pantry at all times. Avocado oil doesn't impart any flavor, making it ideal for baking. If you can't find avocado oil, any neutral cooking oil can be used instead.

NONSTICK SPRAY

I spray my baking pans with coconut oil spray or avocado oil nonstick spray instead of buttering and flouring them because it's easier. Regular nonstick spray can be used (like PAM) but stay away from "baking sprays" as they are not gluten-free and usually contain flour. I've also included a recipe for a gluten-free and dairy-free pan release (page 180) in this book for those who prefer to avoid aerosol products. You can use it to grease your loaf pan for any of these breads as well as for cakes, brownies, muffins and Bundt cakes.

CHOCOLATE

There are several brands of dairy-free chocolate on the market, but I generally use Enjoy Life Foods, because I can easily find it at local grocery stores. Their products are Top-8 free, meaning they don't contain any of the eight most common food allergens, including gluten-containing grains and dairy. For the recipes in this cookbook, I use their chocolate chunks, semi-sweet mini chips and rice milk chocolate bars.

BAKING POWDER

I use Rumford Baking Powder, which is aluminum-free, in all of my gluten-free baked goods. It's available almost anywhere, and I never use anything else. Be sure to check the expiration dates on your baking powder and baking soda to make sure they're not old.

COCOA POWDER

Dutch processed cocoa powder is my go-to cocoa powder in gluten-free baked goods. It's got an intense chocolate flavor that I prefer over regular unsweetened cocoa powder. My absolute favorite is Rodelle Baking Cocoa.

HOW TO MEASURE FLOUR

This may seem like a no-brainer to some, but it's one of the most important tips you can follow when it comes to baking. Using the right amount of flour is crucial to baking successfully.

To properly measure your flour, use the "Spoon and Sweep" method. Start by stirring your flour. Flour settles as it sits, so this step is essential. Use a spoon to scoop the flour into your measuring cup until it is slightly over-filled. Use a straight-edge, like the back of a butter knife, to level off the flour. This will leave the perfect amount in your cup.

You can also measure your ingredients by weight, which will give you the most accurate results.

BATTER CONSISTENCY AND SHAPING YOUR LOAF

The quick breads in this cookbook all have batters thin enough to pour, though the consistency varies (the chocolate-based batters tend to be thicker). They should not be sticky or tacky like you would find with gluten-free yeast breads and should resemble cake batter.

Some of the breads that have a thick batter consistency can be shaped. This is completely optional but gives you a little more control over how the quick bread will look when it's finished baking. To shape your breads, use a spatula to gently mound the batter closer to the middle of the pan. Place the spatula between the batter and the bread pan and gently pull it up towards the middle, giving it a mounded look. Use a sharp knife to cut a deep slit down the center of the bread.

REASONS YOUR BREAD MIGHT BE DRY

The quick breads in this book should be moist. If your breads are coming out too dry, make sure you're measuring your flour correctly.

Cutting too much of the sugar from a recipe can also be a culprit. Sugar, especially brown sugar, plays a role in the moisture level in these breads. While you can reduce the sugar in some of the recipes in this book, I wouldn't cut back more than ¼ to ½ cup (49 to 97 g) at the absolute most to make sure your breads maintain their optimal moisture level.

Baking with the "convection" or "convection baking" setting on your oven can also dry out your baked goods. Stick with the regular, old-fashioned baking setting on your oven.

Baking at a high altitude could also impact the moisture level in your quick breads. If you're baking at a high altitude, be sure to read the High-Altitude Baking section below.

HIGH-ALTITUDE BAKING

If you're baking higher than 2,500 feet (762 m) above sea level, you may need to make some adjustments. Baked goods rise faster and lose moisture faster at higher altitudes; they also take longer to cook all the way through. Depending on the recipe, you may need to bake a little bit longer.

If your altitude is greater than 5,000 feet (1,524 m) above sea level, you may need to make additional adjustments to the amount of liquid or leavening agents used in the recipe. There are plenty of charts available online for free to help you. Some good sites that have free online high-altitude baking guides are kingarthurflour.com, epicurious.com, betterhomesandgardens.com and craftsy.com.

HOW TO BAKE QUICK BREAD BATTER AS MUFFINS

Quick bread batter translates well into muffins because the process and ingredients are almost identical. These bread recipes may make between 12 to 18 muffins, depending on the recipe you use.

To bake the bread as muffins, spray your muffin tins with nonstick spray or coat with homemade pan release (page 180). Prepare the bread as directed and then transfer the batter to the prepared muffin tins, filling them ⅔ of the way full.

Bake your muffins at 400°F (204°C) for 14 to 20 minutes. Baking time will depend greatly on the recipe used. The citrus recipes tend to bake faster, around 14 to 15 minutes. The batters with more moisture or mix-ins, like pumpkin, banana, sweet potato, morning glory, etc., take between 15 to 20 minutes.

Start checking your muffins for doneness around 15 minutes before adding time so you don't over-bake them.

HOW TO BAKE MINI BREADS

While there is only one recipe in this cookbook that actually calls for the breads to be baked in mini loaf pans, you can turn any of these quick breads into mini breads. Simply replace the 9 x 5–inch (23 x 13–cm) loaf pan with 4 mini loaf pans instead.

Coat with nonstick spray and line with parchment paper as you would for a standard loaf. Bake the mini breads for 35 to 45 minutes or until a tester comes out clean. Baking time will depend upon the moisture level in the breads and your oven. I recommend testing at the 35-minute mark before adding additional baking time.

ACKNOWLEDGMENTS

I think I'm still in a bit of disbelief that I've actually done this. Writing a cookbook is something that I've wanted to do for a long time, and I can't believe I can call myself an author. I think I'm also in a bit of disbelief that I was able to do this while also running my business and being a stay-at-home mom. I think I might need a week of sleep to catch up, but you know kids—that won't happen any time soon!

But that's not to say that I've done this all on my own. While writing this cookbook has been one of the hardest and most challenging projects I've ever worked on, it also came with a lot of help. That help is what made this book possible.

First and foremost, I'd like to say thank you to my readers. Thank you for coming back over and over again to make my recipes. It is truly an honor and my pleasure to share gluten-free recipes with you, recipes that my family loves and that I hope your families will love as well. Thank you for your support and encouragement, for your recipe ideas and for cheering me on when recipe development didn't go as planned. Thank you for truly caring about me and for your continued support and following. What the Fork Food Blog wouldn't be what it is today without you.

Thank you to my parents and my grandparents for being the best kind of role models. For showing me the importance of family, love and hard work. And to my grandmother and mom who taught me how to bake and that homemade is always from the heart. For showing me that family truly is more important than anything and that time spent with your family is worth its weight in gold.

Thank you to my husband for all your support and for encouraging me to pursue my goals and dreams. For not letting me settle and keeping me reaching for the stars. For believing in me even when it was hard to believe in myself and for being the rock of our family, even when you don't know you are.

Thank you to Kelsey and Mackenzie, my tiny sous-chefs. I absolutely love baking with you and it's my hope that you'll still want to bake with me even as you grow older and think you're too cool to hang out with me. You make the cutest hand models, and I love capturing your little fingers reaching for the food we made together.

Thank you to my army of recipe testers. For all the time, ingredients and love you put into making sure these recipes were right. I truly appreciate you. From the bottom of my humble heart, I can't thank you enough.

Thank you to Page Street and Caitlin, my editor. Without you, this cookbook would still just be a pipedream. Thank you for turning my dreams into reality.

ABOUT THE AUTHOR

Sharon is the creator of What The Fork Food Blog, which features easy gluten-free baked goods, gluten-free desserts and no-bake treats. Her recipes have been featured on websites like Parade, Redbook, The Huffington Post, Country Living, Fitness Magazine, Cosmopolitan, Shape, Brit + Co., MSN and more. Sharon is also an award-winning food photographer who lives in Connecticut with her husband Adam, two young daughters and three crazy fur-babies, Rocco, Brady and Chaz. Hungry for more? Visit Sharon at whattheforkfoodblog.com, which has been recognized as one of the top gluten-free food blogs every year since 2015.

INDEX